Guidance for Every Child

Guidance for Every Child

Teaching Young Children to Manage Conflict

Dan Gartrell, EdD

Redleaf Press®
www.redleafpress.org
800-423-8309

Published by Redleaf Press
10 Yorkton Court
St. Paul, MN 55117
www.redleafpress.org

First edition 2017
Cover design by Amy Fastenau
Cover photographs/illustrations by iStock.com/Vectoring
Interior design by Jim Handrigan and Douglas Schmitz
Typeset in Utopia and Gora
Printed in the United States of America

Excerpt from *Education for a Civil Society: How Guidance Teaches Young Children Democratic Life Skills* by
Dan Gartrell. Copyright © 2012 NAEYC®. Reprinted with permission.

Selections from Guidance Matters columns, published in *Young Children*, all by Dan Gartrell included in
this book (except where noted):

"'You Really Worked Hard on Your Picture': Guiding with Encouragement." Copyright © 2007 NAEYC®.
   Reprinted with permission.

"Children Who Have Serious Conflicts, Part One." Copyright © 2011 NAEYC®. Reprinted with permission.

"Children Who Have Serious Conflicts, Part Two." Copyright © 2011 NAEYC®. Reprinted with permission.

"Aggression, the Prequel: Preventing the Need." Copyright © 2011 NAEYC®. Reprinted with permission.

"From Rules to Guidelines: Moving to the Positive." Copyright © 2012 NAEYC®. Reprinted with permission.

"Democratic Life Skill Four: Accepting Unique Human Qualities in Others." Copyright © 2013 NAEYC®.
   Reprinted with permission.

"Promote Physical Activity: It's Proactive Guidance" by Dan Gartrell and K. Sonsteng. Copyright © 2008
   NAEYC®. Reprinted with permission.

"Guidance with Girls" by Dan Gartrell and L. Cole. Copyright © 2014 NAEYC®. Reprinted with permission.

Library of Congress Cataloging-in-Publication Data

Names: Gartrell, Daniel, author.
Title: Guidance for every child : teaching young children to manage conflict
   / Dan Gartrell, EdD.
Description: First edition. | St. Paul, MN : Redleaf Press, [2017] | Includes
   bibliographical references and index.
Identifiers: LCCN 2017000650 (print) | LCCN 2017018766 (ebook) | ISBN
   9781605545387 (ebook) | ISBN 9781605545370 (pbk. : acid-free paper)
Subjects: LCSH: School discipline. | Conflict management--Study and teaching
   (Early childhood)
Classification: LCC LB3012 (ebook) | LCC LB3012 .G39 2017 (print) | DDC
   372.15/8--dc23
LC record available at https://lccn.loc.gov/2017000650

Printed on acid-free paper

U20-03

*In memory of my longtime mentor at Bemidji State University,
Emeritus Professor of Education Dr. Charles Austad.
Thank you, Chuck, for being interested in my writing.*

Contents

Acknowledgments

FIRST, I WOULD LIKE TO ACKNOWLEDGE MY MOTHER, Beth Goff, who in her seventies self-published a remarkable memoir, *Understanding Backwards*, and in her eighties had her story used in a National Public Radio anthology on long-ago friendships lost and refound. Her memory keeps me writing as I approach her age at the time of her later publications.

And I extend special gratitude to my wife, Dr. Julie Jochum Gartrell, for her good guidance and friendship around the writing I have wanted and needed to do over the last thirty years.

I have had the privilege of working with several colleague-friends who have been coauthors and supportive editors of articles, sections of books, and some of my Guidance Matters columns in *Young Children*. They have shared with me their particular expertise, writing skills, and general early childhood wisdom. I have benefited from working with each of them. They include

Karen Cairone	Brian Nelson
Layna Cole	Leah Pigatti
Michael Gallo	June Reinike
Lynn Gerhke	Kathleen Sonsteng
Margaret King	

To each of them, many thanks.

Thanks also go to the publishers and editors over the years who accepted my submissions and guided me in many matters of writing, publishing, and editing. At Cengage Learning, they include Mark Kerr and the editorial teams that have seen me through six editions of my textbook, *A Guidance Approach for the Encouraging Classroom*.

At NAEYC, four persons who have assisted me are Derry Koralek, Amy Shilady, Kathleen Charner, and Polly Greenberg. Derry got me started with the Guidance Matters column in *Young Children*, which ran from 2005 through 2014; Amy was my editor on several NAEYC projects; and Kathleen, in charge of book publications, was a firm supporter during the development of *Education for a Civil Society*. I hold special gratitude for Polly Greenberg, who published my first article in *Young Children* back in 1987, and at six o'clock that New Year's Eve, edited, *over the phone*, my first Viewpoint piece: "Assertive Discipline: Unhealthy for Children and

Other Living Things." On the heels of the first article, this one—which I know Polly enjoyed working on—appeared in the March 1988 issue of *Young Children*.

The piece stirred up quite a commotion nationally among the Assertive Discipline crowd. In my town of Bemidji, Minnesota, after the piece appeared in the local newspaper, school officials banned me from supervising student teachers there. Two principals even visited the vice president at Bemidji State University and tried unsuccessfully to persuade him not to grant me tenure. (I am still grateful that Dr. Les Duly kindly ushered them out of his office. He had read the article. May the trees planted by the memorial to Dr. Duly continue to bloom beautifully.) The ban was rescinded after the superintendent left. I hope the two principals are enjoying their retirements as much as I am.

Appreciation is expressed to Carole White and her crew at *Exchange Magazine* for publishing three of my articles in late 2015 and early 2016. The first two articles are adapted here as chapters 1 and 2 and serve as the foundation for this book. The third article has my favorite title of all I have ever used: "Developmentally Appropriate STEM: It's STREAM!" (STREAM stands for Science, Technology, Relationships, Engineering, Arts, and Mathematics—a term that Thea Blair shared with me in 2014.)

At Redleaf Press, gratitude is extended to Beth Wallace, editor of my first book published at Redleaf, *What the Kids Said Today*. Of course, I also want to thank the Redleaf staff who have worked patiently with this old professor-dude on the present book, especially manager of content development Laurie Herrmann; acquisitions and developmental editor Kara Lomen; editor Andrea Rud; and managing editor Douglas Schmitz. I trust that their open-mindedness and quiet competence show in the pages that follow. If not, it is only because I have been too slow a learner.

Some of these same publishing folks deserve appreciative recognition for granting permission to reproduce in this book excerpts from previous publications, including my Cengage/Wadsworth text, books and columns for NAEYC, articles in *Exchange Magazine,* and several anecdotes from *What the Kids Said Today.* Many thanks to Mark, Kathy, Carole, and Laura.

Lasting appreciation is conveyed to the early childhood professionals who have been my good colleagues over the years, including many former students from my nearly forty years of teaching early childhood professionals-to-be at Bemidji State. They have shared with me anecdotes, experiences, and "comfortable shoes on the floor" knowledge that have made much of what I have written possible. I want to recognize in particular three former students: practicing and retired teachers Sharon Hoverson in Ponemah, Minnesota, and Robin Bakken and Pat Sanford in Bemidji, Minnesota. You will see the vignettes and quotes attributed to them.

To the early childhood professionals long ago at the Red Lake Nation Head Start and not so long ago at the Mahube Head Start program in northwestern Minnesota, I convey my never-ending gratitude for modeling good guidance, both intuitive and intentional, with their children.

And finally, I'd like to thank you many readers who are using guidance with every child. You, more than teachers at any other level, make a difference in the presents and futures of the little ones with whom you share your lives during this critical time in their development.

Julie and I are members of a blended family that includes five children, eleven grandchildren, and one great-grandchild. I am blessed by each and every family member, and I know the adage said in many ways is true: Grandchildren (and great-grandchildren) are God's reward for not having alienated your kids. Ideally, families provide the encouraging environment that allows writing and many other good things to happen. In my case, this is true.

Dan Gartrell
Bemidji, Minnesota
www.dangartrell.net

Introduction

FOR NEARLY FIFTY YEARS I have been in the learning settings of infants, toddlers, preschoolers, kindergartners, primary children, and early childhood teacher-education students. In my various roles as a teacher, CDA trainer, college professor, student teacher, supervisor, and consultant adviser, I have observed countless adult-child interactions that have inspired me for their amazing humanity. This book is a reflective celebration of positive teacher-child interactions in early childhood settings, and of the relationships and teaching practices to which these interactions attest. From my first year of teaching Head Start for the Red Lake Band of Ojibwe in northern Minnesota, this memorable story illustrates what I mean:

 After a few weeks of Head Start, a three-year-old named Jimmy began to look for the teacher each day upon arrival in order to give her a kick in the leg! Sue, a first-year teacher, tried everything she could think of from her classroom management book. After a few days of this repeated behavior, Sue was about to contact the parent when other staff members indicated that Jimmy might then be severely punished at home. Giving the matter (considerable) thought, on Thursday, as soon as Jimmy entered the room, Sue said, "Jimmy, I am so pleased to see you in school today!" As she said this, she knelt down and gave him a great big hug! Sue repeated the strategy on Friday. When Jimmy came into class the following Monday, he looked for Sue, waved, and said, "Hi, Teach, I'm here." Four years later, Sue received a Christmas card from Jimmy and his mother. Sue shared the note inside with me: "Hi, Teach, I am having a nice Christmas. I hope you are too. I still remember you. Do you remember me?"

Children at Risk

In current early childhood care and education, it has been my experience that most teachers easily build positive relationships with perhaps 80 percent of a typical group of young learners. (Eighty percent is approximately the number of American youth who graduate from high school each year with their peers [US Department of Education 2015].) Karen Cairone (2016) points out that in some settings, the number of "easily likable" young children may be as high as 95 percent. In others, largely due to the challenges of poverty, it may be as low as 40 percent. (Only about 40 percent of American black males graduated from high school with their peers in 2014 [Schott Foundation for Public Education 2015].) The 80 percent or 40 percent can basically meet the (written and unwritten) standards for conduct and performance expected in the classroom. It is the other 20 percent, the other 60 percent who try the teacher's personal resources.

Due to their atypical behaviors, activity levels, and learning styles, these children are at risk of marginal acceptance, if not overt rejection, by adults in the learning setting. Other children in the group take note of repeated incidents of public corrective reactions toward these youngsters, and they may steer clear of them out of safety concerns or in deference to the teacher's apparent views toward the singled-out children (Ladd 2006).

Rejection of children is a serious problem in early childhood programs. In 2005, 2006, and again in 2012, national studies showed that expulsion rates in preschools were much higher than in K–12 education. In the Gilliam studies (Gilliam 2005; Gilliam and Shahar 2006), four out of five children expelled were boys; a majority were children of color older than thirty-six months. For children rejected in preschool, unsuccessful education outcomes become likely (Ladd 2006). Gaining at best a sputtering start to their educational lives, too many of these children leave schools prematurely or endure years of unhappy schooling (Ettekal and Ladd 2015). The 60 percent of American black males who do not graduate, I believe, provide testimony to this widespread pattern of rejection in the classroom and educational failure. Too often the pattern begins in early childhood.

Guidance, Not Discipline

The entrenched cultural baggage of traditional classroom discipline has meant that discipline too easily slides into punishment. Some adults in early childhood programs have failed to discard the centuries-old notion that they can shame a child into being "good." With young children, *punishment*, the infliction of pain and suffering on individuals as a consequence of something they have done, just plain doesn't work (Copple and Bredekamp 2009).

Brain research now tells us that when children cause serious classroom conflicts, they are reacting to high stress levels—that is, toxic stress—that they cannot otherwise manage (Shonkoff and Garner 2011). The conflict these children cause and fall into are mistaken efforts to protect themselves and relieve the stress. While they may feel an adrenaline rush during the conflict (that masks the stress), punishment results in further stress that remains unmanageable. Sitting on the age-old time-out chair, they are *not* thinking, "I am going to be a better child because Teacher has temporarily expelled me from the group!" At a sensitized emotional level, they are feeling, "Teacher doesn't like me. I can't think how to act better! I am worthless. I don't like it here." In a well-received meta-analysis, Gunnar, Herrera, and Hostinar (2009) document a cycle of

feeling unmanageable stress,

reacting to the stress by causing conflict

resulting in punishment and rejection by others

leading to self-debasement and continued stress.

Consistent across the studies analyzed, the authors found that this *stress-rejection cycle* has a long-term devastating effect on young human beings.

It is noteworthy that recent editions of NAEYC's Developmentally Appropriate Practice in Programs Serving Children from Birth through Age 8 (Copple and Bredekamp 2009) have minimized use of the term discipline. Instead, at every age level addressed in this hallowed work, references are made to using guidance. In the broad view, guidance is teaching for healthy emotional and social development; my day-to-day definition holds that guidance is teaching children to learn from their mistakes rather than punishing them for their mistakes. Guidance is teaching children how to solve their problems rather than punishing them for having problems that are bigger than they are, problems that they haven't learned to solve on their own yet. Guidance prevents harm in the classroom, so it is firm when it needs to be. But guidance is firm and friendly, not firm and harsh.

Important here is the idea that teachers who use guidance see young children as being only months old. A three-year-old like Jimmy has fewer than forty-eight months of life experience. At the beginning of a lifelong process of learning very difficult skills, young children naturally make mistakes in their behavior and cause conflicts, on occasion spectacularly. It is the positive relationship between the adult and these months-old beings that helps them keep stress manageable, grow in their ability to trust, and increase their capacity to get along. Guidance always builds from secure adult-child relationships, using this foundation to help the child gain emotional-social skills.

Notice that I speak of emotional-social skills and not the other way around. To paraphrase a twentieth-century psychologist influential in my writings, a child must feel right in order to think and do right (Ginott 1993). In a guidance approach, emotional well-being comes first. Children can accept others only when they can accept themselves.

Guidance and Developmentally Appropriate Practice

For me, developmentally appropriate practice (DAP) means guiding each child in an education that is in harmony with the unique developmental dynamic within that child. In early childhood education today, teachers feel profoundly contradictory pressures: on the one hand, to use developmentally appropriate practice, and on the other hand, to use traditional school-socialization practices in order to get children ready for anticipated behavioral and academic expectations ahead. Every day, early childhood teachers experience energetic children still learning kinetically like all young mammals: through movement, physical exploration, and spontaneous social interactions. At the same time, these teachers feel pressures to ready these naturally active children for the anticipated sit-down, follow-directions, pencil-and-paper instructional activities taught through prolonged sedentary time blocks at the next level. Sound familiar? In the words of Pat Sanford, my colleague–kindergarten teacher, "It is not my job to prepare children for the next level. It is my job to give each child the best possible kindergarten (or prekindergarten) experience they can have."

In early childhood education at its best, this developmental understanding extends to children who might have difficulty fitting into traditionally operated programs. The matter comes down to the teacher-child relationship. Contrary to a common myth, early childhood teachers do not need to love every child they work with. However, as caring professionals, they do need to forge positive relationships with every child. An illustration of the positive relationships early childhood professionals build with children every day is Viola's story.

 On the single main street of a town in northwestern Minnesota, veteran preschool teacher Viola was walking toward her car. She heard, "Viola, Viola!" behind her. A smiling young woman came up to her and said, "My name is Nancy Peterson. You probably don't remember me. I had you as my preschool teacher, and ever since then I wanted to be a teacher myself. I am now in the University of North Dakota early childhood education program! I just want to thank you."

Viola and Nancy exchanged more friendly words, and Viola maybe wiped away a tear. After the two parted and Viola was getting into her car, she suddenly remembered Nancy. "That kid?" Nancy's ceaseless energy and independence had driven Viola bonkers every day of that classroom year. But because of the relationship Viola built with her, Nancy never knew.

From a *proactive positive relationship* with a child comes a teacher's motivation to figure out how to accommodate the child's unique pattern of behavior and learning, including how to modify the program. Only then does the program become truly developmentally appropriate, for—in my view—a program is only developmentally appropriate when it is DA for every child in the group.

It is my experience that early childhood programs become developmentally appropriate for children when they operate like good summer camps. Adults in these active and creative settings do not feel compelled to enforce academic and behavioral standards they know to be inappropriate. Instead, teachers in these settings build relationships responsive to the children's needs and developmental circumstances—leading to whole-child, developmentally appropriate learning experiences. Curriculum in developmentally appropriate programs tends to be emergent, not rigidly preset, and teachers act not as technicians, but as guidance professionals. These professionals do assess children's progress to be sure, but they do so through minimally invasive, authentic assessment, which does not dictate inappropriate content and teaching methods.

About This Book

The topics in the chapters that follow cluster around building on proactive positive relationships with every young child in the group. Having worked often with short-form writing—articles, columns, pieces for encyclopedias, etc.—I intend for every chapter to be its own essay. By this, I mean that each chapter starts with information from preceding chapters and recasts that information from a new perspective. To the extent that the approach works, at the end of each chapter, the reader should have a clear picture of a particular dimension of guidance practice in early learning settings.

Also, readers should know that the book reworks material from my NAEYC writings over the years—writings that focused on teaching conflict management skills to young children through positive teacher-child relationships. We can call the work a retrospective if you'd like, a bringing together in one place of several important guidance ideas I've worked with, presented as a hopefully clear over-view. For new readers, my wish is that these ideas have personal meaning for you. For veteran readers of my works, I hope you consider the book a reinforcement of important concepts—and not just the old-dude professor carrying on about the same old things. My fate is in your hands.

Vignettes

As readers of the Guidance Matters columns know, I use vignettes to illustrate the ideas I discuss. These anecdotes help ideas come alive. The vignettes in this book begin with actual experiences, either mine or documented by colleagues. From time to time I change names or add a detail to make a point, but the vignettes all essentially happened as I represent them. In addition, each chapter contains numerous references to the scholarly works of other authors; this is my effort to connect the concepts discussed to accepted core ideas in our field.

People sometimes contact me to share their stories, and I am always pleased when this happens. After they swear on their Good Book that the incident hap-pened as they describe, it goes in my electronic notebook for possible future use. "For a short time only, present company is included in this special offer!" (Notice there is no expiration date.)

Friendly Humor

In your years as a student, you probably witnessed teachers using sarcastic humor to put individuals or groups in their place. Embarrassment is likely the most common form of punishment teachers use to control situations and students. *Friendly* humor is different, laughing with children, not at them. It is a good thing to smile discreetly when a child says something unexpected and charming—even when what they say may not be appropriate in adult life. Teachers should just plain grin when a child is asked to use the magic words, and he responds with, "Abra-cadabra!" Or when a child in conflict is told to use her words, and she exclaims, "I can't find any!" Certainly, a teacher should chuckle when she says it's raining cats and dogs outside, which results in the reply from a preschooler, "And elephants even!" The modeling and support of friendly humor can awaken the latent sense of humor in every child—to my thinking, a lifelong gift and strength.

I use humor in this book not always adroitly but always in well-intended ways. Friendly humor lightens situations and lessens stress, tension, and concentration fatigue. It builds human connections, and it can add that spoonful of honey that helps interventions go down. If one cannot smile often in the presence of young children, I suggest considering a new profession, maybe IT. Just remember, if something goes exactly the way you expect with young children, something is wrong. So smile and enjoy the kids . . . and they will enjoy being with you.

Key Guidance Constructs

Along with guidance itself, four other integral constructs appear in several chapters. They are Mistaken Behavior; Three Levels of Mistaken Behavior; Five Democratic Life Skills; and Liberation Teaching.

Mistaken Behavior. From birth to death, all humans experience *conflicts*, expressed disagreements between individuals. Life is replete with conflict—it is part of being alive. When people are fortunate or at their best, they resolve their conflicts peacefully. In learning the skills of conflict management, young children, who are just beginners, make mistakes in their judgments and show mistaken behaviors.

Three Levels of Mistaken Behavior. For almost half a century, I have used this construct to help explain why children show mistaken behaviors. The levels correspond to degrees of mental health in children. The levels, in order of decreasing mental health, are

Level one, experimentation mistaken behavior. A child who is open to new experiences tries something; it doesn't work, and a conflict occurs. Emotions might be raw at the moment, but the child at level one reconciles fairly quickly and moves on to other new experiences.

Level two, socially influenced mistaken behavior. Children may be making progress with insecurities and stress, but they defer to significant others as authority figures in their behavior. For reasons of perceived safety, they go along to get along, as the saying goes. Children at level two are easily influenced by others, which can lead to classroom conflicts.

Level three, strong-unmet-needs mistaken behavior. Children are experiencing the strong motivation of unmet basic needs, and the resulting stress affects their outlooks and reaction tendencies across time. The conflicts they are involved in tend to be extreme and repeated. These children are at risk for falling into the stress-rejection cycle.

Five Democratic Life Skills. The five democratic life skills (DLS) represent skills that people need to function in and contribute to a modern, complex, democratic society. The first two skills indicate that the individual is working on the primary motivational source, for safety and security. This two-skill set must be largely gained before the child can work effectively on the next three skills, which pertain to the secondary motivation source, for psychological growth. The five democratic life skills are as follows:

1. Finding acceptance as a worthy member of the group and as an individual

2. Expressing strong emotions in nonhurting ways

3. Solving problems creatively—independently and in cooperation with others

4. Accepting unique human qualities in others

5. Thinking intelligently and ethically

Children who have not yet gained DLS 1 and 2 are at risk for showing level three mistaken behavior. As they make progress in gaining these basic needs-related skills and are beginning to move to the next three, they are more apt to show mistaken behavior at levels two and one.

Liberation Teaching. *Liberation teaching* means never giving up on any child. It is the practice of guidance at its purest and best. With respect to the democratic life skills, liberation teaching means providing the positive leadership children need to gain DLS 1 and 2 and make progress in gaining DLS 3, 4, and 5. With respect to the three levels of mistaken behavior, liberation teaching means teaming with the child, family, and caregivers to make strong-unmet-needs mistaken behavior unnecessary.

Discussion Questions and Key Concepts

At the end of each chapter, a small number of *discussion questions* provide the opportunity to further study guidance concepts and practices. Most of the questions ask the reader to reflect about real-life experiences from the context of chapter ideas. In discussing the questions with colleagues, privacy considerations are important here. For me, such questions help make the content of each chapter viable and real. It is my hope that the reader finds this to be true as well.

Key concepts are featured terms in each chapter; they provide a vocabulary that helps to explain and understand the guidance approach. I rely on key concepts in my writings to help readers engage with guidance concepts and practices and to raise awareness of teaching practices that calm and guide rather than punish. A list of key concepts appears at the end of each chapter, and you will find the terms defined in the glossary at the end of the book.

Guidance means that during conflicts, adults calm and teach rather than punish; this way children learn alternatives to hurting behaviors that they can use in the future when they experience conflicts. In moving to a guidance approach, it is important to remember that young children are eminently social beings who internalize and learn from the behaviors of the peers and adults around them. When early childhood professionals model and teach the attitudes and skills of a caring, inclusive community, children internalize this learning. In settings where children see adults actively guiding and caring about children who have difficult life circumstances, helping them to feel accepted and valued, they gain in the emotional-social capacities that our society so clearly needs. This is my central message, one that I hope readers also aspire to and gain in understanding about as we travel together through the pages of this book.

Discussion Questions

An element of being an early childhood professional is respecting the children, parents, and educators you are working with by keeping identities private. In completing follow-up activities, please respect the privacy of all concerned.

1. Think about a child who was challenging for you or a colleague to get to know and work with. Talk about progress made in building a positive relationship with this child and in helping the child to adjust to the learning setting. What are one or two ideas from the chapter that you can relate to this experience?

2. In relation to your or your colleagues' work with this child, what are you most pleased and most frustrated with? What are some lessons learned from working with this child? What are one or two ideas from the chapter that might help you in a similar experience in the future?

3. Think about a child who had a difficult time in a learning setting one year and a better time the following year. Discuss the nature of the different teachers' relationships with this child during the two periods. What effect do you think the differing relationships had on the child's emotional and academic outcomes during the two periods? What do you conclude about the importance of the teacher-child relationship from this experience?

Key Concepts

Definitions of the Key Concepts can be found in the glossary on pages 177–84.

Conflicts	**Proactive positive relationships**
Five democratic life skills	**Stress-rejection cycle**
Friendly humor	**Three levels of mistaken behavior**
Guidance	**Toxic stress**
Mistaken behavior	

CHAPTER 1

Challenging Behaviors Mean Challenged Children

PSYCHOLOGISTS WHO STUDY BRAIN DEVELOPMENT ARE validating what caring teachers have known for years: there is no such thing as bad kids, only kids with bad problems that they cannot solve on their own (Cozolino 2006). This chapter looks at key sources of children's problems and how these problems cause young children to show behaviors that are challenging. Subsequent chapters illustrate individual- and group-focused guidance practices that help young children manage their problems and gain the emotional and social strengths that help them get along.

Building from the discussion in the introduction, three basic ideas will guide our conversation throughout the book. First, early childhood professionals do well to think of young children not as years old, but as months old. Adults sometimes expect emotional maturity from young children during conflicts that even we adults, with years of life experience, do not always show.

Second, we use the term *guidance* to define developmentally appropriate leadership with children who show challenging behaviors (Gartrell 2014). In immediate situations, guidance means intervening in conflicts in firm but friendly ways that calm and teach rather than punish. In the larger sense, guidance is teaching for healthy emotional and social development.

Third, early childhood professionals build and sustain *proactive positive relationships* with every child in the group, even during conflicts. Proactive means that the adult accepts responsibility for the viability of the relationship for the entire time the child and the child's family are in the program. Proactive positive relationships extend beyond the child to the family, beginning with the teacher's first contact with family members.

Thanks to *Exchange Magazine* for permission to adapt my article in the September–October 2015 issue for this chapter.

Looking at the ideas together, with limited experience and rapid but still early brain development, young children show only the beginnings of emotional-social competence. Because they are just beginning a complex, lifelong learning process, children frequently make mistakes in their behavior. Teachers who have adopted this guidance perspective view the conflicts that children have not as misbehavior, but as mistaken behavior. Thus, when adults take a guidance approach, they help children learn from their mistakes rather than punish them for their mistakes. They help children learn to solve their problems rather than punish them for having problems that they have not yet learned how to solve. Guidance is based on, and always endeavors to build, positive adult-child and adult-adult relationships.

Stress and Behavior

From the writings of Montessori and Froebel in Europe, to mid-twentieth-century American psychologists Maslow, Ainsworth, and Bowlby, to current brain development research, the encouraging adult-child relationship has been established as the foundation of a child's healthy emotional-social development. This section takes us through the findings of these twentieth-century psychologists and recent brain research to identify the fundamental causes of mistaken behaviors in early childhood learning settings.

Maslow's Two Sources of Internal Motivation

Before the time of physiology-based brain study, the psychologist Abraham Maslow (1962) famously identified a hierarchy of needs and two sources of internal motivation that drive the need to fulfill those needs. The first source of motivation, particularly powerful in the young, is for physical and emotional safety: freedom from threats including abuse and neglect, persecution from outside the family, hunger and housing insecurity, and dysfunctional attachments with family members.

With pressing safety needs met, infants and young children are freed from existential stress and can respond to Maslow's second source of motivation: for learning and psychological growth. Rather than show the often-challenging survival behaviors of children who are unable to meet safety needs, children who are able to respond to the intrinsic learning and growth motivation show an amazing capacity for initiative in new situations and for learning in fundamentally healthy emotional, social, cognitive, and physical ways. Preschooler Ansha exemplifies a child who is able to respond to growth-needs motivation. Notice Ansha's use of intelligent and ethical thinking (democratic life skill five) in her response to her friend Lena:

 Ansha is fifty-six months old. On a Friday afternoon at preschool, Ansha's dear friend Lena went home with long dark hair. Monday morning, after a weekend in her older sister's care, Lena walked into the classroom with a blue buzz cut! Lena asked Ansha what she thought of her haircut. Ansha started to say something but changed her mind, replying instead, "I am still getting used to it." "Me too," said Lena, and the two went off to play. Ansha's intelligent and ethical reply taught the adults in this situation what to say (!), and it indicates the motivational source of the child's behavior. (The staff later talked with Lena's parents. They learned that Lena's older sister had just begun cosmetology classes and apparently used Lena for "practice.") Fortunately for Lena, she had Ansha for a friend.

Attachment Theory

In the two decades following Maslow's publications, John Bowlby and Mary Ainsworth documented that the primary dynamic in helping infants and young children meet their safety needs is a *secure attachment* with at least one significant family member. Taking a clinic-centered approach, Bowlby (1982) demonstrated a firm connection between a positive, predictable mother-child attachment in the first years of life and the growing young child's confidence, competence, and sociability in new situations.

Pursuing research similar to Bowlby's, Ainsworth (1978) determined that the attachment style of the mother predicts the coping abilities of the growing child. Ainsworth identified three attachment styles: secure, ambivalent, and avoidant. She found that children securely attached to a parent are less disruptive and aggressive and more empathetic than children experiencing attachments marked by ambivalence or avoidance on the part of the adult. Bowlby and Ainsworth increased our understanding of why children become possessed by, or are able to rise above, the drive to meet basic safety needs. Children who are deprived of a sense of trust and belonging in adult-child relationships experience unmanageable stress and become totally occupied with meeting their safety needs. In contrast, children in secure relationships with significant others have safety needs that are being fulfilled; they view the world as relatively nonthreatening and inviting of exploration.

In the Age of Brain Research

Since the 1990s, amazing new equipment for studying brain activity has enabled neuropsychologists to document and assess the brain's physiological responses to outside stimuli (Elliot 2003). These neuropsychologists have found two basic brain dynamics that help explain the the two motivational drives theorized by Maslow. The brain research also supports the validity of *attachment theory* (Cozolino 2006).

The first dynamic develops early in life to help the infant react to perceived threats (which the infant processes as stress). Robust crying is the primary expression of this dynamic. The amygdala is the brain center that regulates threat perception and the consequent hormonal and bodily reactions to it. *Survival behaviors*, known as fight, freeze, or flee behaviors, are the classic result of amygdala-driven reactions to perceived threats (Gunnar, Herrera, and Hostinar 2009). In this sense, a baby's crying is considered a fight reaction—regardless of the circumstances, the infant gives full voice to discomfort.

By about age three, a second collection of more complex processes called *executive functions* begin to develop within the brain's frontal lobes (Elliot 2003). (Executive functions do not operate with maturity until individuals reach their twenties.) Executive functions consist of coordinated mental processes that interpret present experiences using memory of prior experience; form concepts and action tendencies; stay on course with intentional responses; perceive the results of the course of action, and continue on with executive functioning.

When young children perceive a threat, the resulting stress hormones cause reactions that overwhelm the beginning operations of executive function (Shonkoff and Garner 2011). Amygdala-driven brain reactions override the more balanced functioning mediated by the frontal lobes. If the threat is severe enough, or if it continues, children feel an elevated stress level that becomes central to their state of mind. These children become oversensitive to threat, perceiving it in everyday situations that seem ordinary to those around them. They show frequent and sometimes extreme fight, freeze, or flee reactions during conflicts, frequently in the form of aggression, which everyone around the child finds challenging (Cairone and Mackrain 2012).

Toxic Stress and Conflicts

It is my view that children who are involved in frequent and serious conflicts in early childhood settings are reacting to unmanageable stress in their lives, what Shonkoff and Garner (2011) call *toxic stress*. In a reaction to toxic stress, young children perceive situations as threatening and show the survival behavior of aggression in a mistaken effort to fend off the real or imagined threat. An example is Alex, who gets too much paint on his paper when another child accidentally bumps his elbow. Alex screams and paints the back of the child as she walks past, then crumples the paper, sits on the floor, and yowls. It is reasonable to guess that unmanageable stress drove Alex to react with this intensity and the paint-on-the-back aggression.

Toxic stress can be the result of environmental factors such as tumultuous life circumstances. A second source of toxic stress is neurological; atypical brain structure and development causes children to feel easily overloaded (stressed) in ordinary situations. Children who experience this internal source of stress often prove difficult to parent and to teach. Environmental frustrations often compound the neurological stress that these children feel.

Environmental Factors and Stress

Hunger, tangible housing insecurity, and/or a perceived threat of harm and abandonment cause toxic stress. Violence within and to the family, experienced or witnessed (even if only once), can cause toxic stress. Lubit (2010) argues that the boundary between toxic stress and childhood post-traumatic stress syndrome is sometimes indistinct. All of us would do well to consider that a child involved in serious classroom conflicts may be experiencing childhood post-traumatic stress syndrome.

A significant factor leading to toxic stress is poverty (CDF 2015). Parents who are struggling to meet basic needs for their families experience high levels of stress themselves. Mental health problems, self-medication, aggression, and relational issues (that is, insecure and avoidant attachments with children) all follow from inadequate family resources.

Environmentally caused stress: During the first week of preschool, Jerome, aged forty-nine months, hit another child in the stomach. One teacher comforted the hurt child while another put Jerome on a time-out chair, "to think about what you have done." After a few minutes, the second teacher talked with Jerome and later read a book with him.

The next week, Jerome again hit a child in the stomach. As the teacher approached him, Jerome walked to the time-out chair and said, "I'm going to the chair 'cause I'm no good." The teacher sat with Jerome and talked with him for a long time. She asked a family service worker about the boy and learned that his mother had gone into drug treatment the previous week; the children in the family had been divided among relatives. Discovering the difficult situation that Jerome was facing, the teacher worked hard to build a close relationship with him, and she later built a relationship with Jerome's mother. With the teacher's assistance, Jerome made improvements in handling his stress and became friendlier to his mates in the classroom.

To move past a stereotype in our discussion, it should be noted that the home environments of families with solid basic resources can also lead to unmanageable stress levels in children. Sudden unemployment, marital discord, abusiveness, unhealthy dependencies of all kinds, and overwhelmed parents (or parent surrogates) are environmental factors that can all lead to children experiencing toxic stress. The complexities of modern family life—for families of all income levels—can lead to mental health issues in one or more family members that negatively affect children's sense of belonging and worth.

Neurological Factors and Stress

Neurologically caused stress is a by-product of atypically developing brains. The diagnoses are out there: autism spectrum disorder, Asperger syndrome, attention deficit/hyperactivity disorder, extreme temperaments, childhood mental illness, and other conditions within the body and brain that make frustration and anxiety come too easily to children's minds.

For the most part, these disorders occur in children regardless of family income and education, though adequate family resources can reduce environmental add-ons to neurologically derived stress. Still, in the challenge of building secure attachments with atypically developing children, two parents with PhDs in psychology may not have the dispositions and reliably positive responsiveness that a single parent without a college degree might have. For families of all walks of life, environmental factors often add to stress caused by the neurological condition, which can make children all the more challenged when they enter the early childhood community.

 Neurologically caused stress: Teachers knew that Ryan, aged forty-one months, had difficulty concentrating during many classroom tasks. When he did engage, Ryan reacted strongly to giving up the activity either for another's turn or because of the daily schedule. Changes in the daily schedule, unless handled in a low-key way, seemed to threaten him.

On this morning, the cleanup bell rang just as Ryan was getting a turn with a long piece of cardboard that he was using as a ramp for his truck. Ryan fell to the ground, pulled the ramp down on top of himself, and began to scream. His teacher calmly explained that it was time for Ryan and the class to go outside; Ryan could use the ramp again afterward. Ryan continued wailing until the teacher asked him if they could put the ramp in a special place so he could be sure to get it when they came in. Ryan immediately stood up and carried the ramp to a spot behind the teacher's table, now smiling.

The teacher made sure Ryan found the ramp as soon as the class returned. Ryan used the ramp for twenty minutes and let two other children use their own vehicles with him.

Sources of Stress within the Learning Setting

The following are key conditions for healthy emotional and social development to flourish in learning settings:

- a welcoming community inclusive of every family, whatever the background

- secure attachments (proactive positive relationships) between adults and each child

- an encouraging learning environment that is developmentally appropriate for every child

- the use of firm but friendly guidance with all children, individually and in groups

- collaborative staff who enjoy working together and who further a whole child/whole community vision of the program

We will explore the creation and utilization of these key conditions in chapters to follow. Important here is that shortcomings in any of the elements lead to what I call *program-caused mistaken behavior*, resulting in undue stress for program members.

As an example, consider a preschool group that has many active children. The schedule calls for an early and lengthy large group each day that includes attendance, calendar, weather, a flannel board story or book, special events, and sometimes a visitor. Most of the children simply cannot sit and listen this long, but the teacher feels it is her duty to socialize the children to circle time. Every morning, children get restless; some get rowdy. The teacher calls names to try to make them refocus and ends up putting some children on time-out chairs—these children then feel the additional stress of conflict with the teacher.

In this instance, the classroom schedule has caused the mistaken behavior—on the part of both the children *and* the teacher. In a developmentally appropriate setting for all children, the early childhood professional would not use circle times in this way; the mistaken behavior, with its emotional side effects, would not occur. (See chapter 3 for further discussion of this matter.)

Of course, conflicts occur in settings that are fully encouraging too, but they need not contribute to children's unmanageable stress. And guidance professionals should not feel they need to prevent all conflicts, anyway; they just need to halt those that might result in harm and children's undue stress. In making the determination as to whether and how to intervene, let's return to the three levels of mistaken behavior discussed in the introduction.

Three Levels of Mistaken Behavior

I give credit to my long-ago faculty adviser at the University of North Dakota, Dr. Stephen D. Harlow, for the fundamental idea that led to the construct of levels of mistaken behavior. Harlow wrote that children's behaviors cluster around one of three levels of relationships in their interactions. The three levels are based on children's psychological progress in meeting safety needs and working on growth needs (1975). My own observation has been that at each level, children are susceptible to characteristic mistakes in their behavior. The resulting three-level construct of mistaken behavior follows.

Level One: Experimentation Mistaken Behavior

Children experience conflicts at level one when they are encountering their worlds openly, bringing self-directed motivation to their everyday activities and interactions. Children show *experimentation mistaken behavior* for two basic reasons. In the first, they are engaged in a situation, it goes in an unintended direction that gets out of hand, and a conflict results. Think of this as an uncontrolled experiment. In the second, they try something intentionally to see what the reaction of others will be, and the reaction is a conflict. Think of this as a controlled experiment.

Here is an illustration of unintentional experimentation mistaken behavior—our uncontrolled experiment.

 Cynthia, a fifty-six-month-old, has easily mastered each of the room's several puzzles. So, she has gotten out five puzzles at once, mixed up the pieces, and is completing all five at the same time! While she is working, it comes time for the group to put things away and go outside. Totally engaged, Cynthia does not notice the transition protocol and keeps working on the puzzles. An adult in the room lectures Cynthia about her stubbornness and failure to follow directions—and tells her she is not doing the puzzles correctly.

Lead teacher Meryl arrives and quietly asks the other adult to take the rest of the group outside. Meryl kneels down and has a guidance talk with the girl. (See chapter 7 for information on guidance talks.) She says how amazed she is that Cynthia can do five puzzles at once. She reminds Cynthia that it is time "to give our bodies exercise outside." She asks if she can tell the other adult that Cynthia will finish the puzzles later during work time. Together they put up a sign that says, "Cynthia is doing these puzzles." She tells Cynthia that because she is so skilled at doing puzzles, she is going to bring in a really complicated puzzle for Cynthia to try. They go outside. The next day, Meryl brings in a forty-piece puzzle, and the two work on it together. Over the next few days, Cynthia works with other children to model and teach how to complete the new big-kid puzzle.

Here is an illustration of intentionally caused level one mistaken behavior—our controlled experiment.

 During rest time, a provider saw Amelia, a very shy forty-eight-month-old, sit up, tug on the hair of the sleeping three-year-old next to her, lie back down, and pretend she was asleep. The sleepy three-year-old sat up, rubbed his head, and lay back down. Recalling the incident later, the provider smiled and told me, "I am glad Amelia is finally feeling comfortable enough here to make a little mischief. If it happens again, I will say something, but this time I am going to let it ride." My thinking exactly.

With experimenting mistaken behavior, the teacher's response makes all the difference. The teacher needs to appreciate that level one mistaken behavior means the child is fully engaged in the experiments of life, is meeting safety needs, and is working on learning and mental growth needs. *Mastery motivation* (the motivation for psychological growth that is organic to the child's mind and body) is at play, a state of mind in the child that the early childhood professional protects and nurtures.

Typically, if early childhood professionals decide to intervene when observing experimentation mistaken behavior, they soft-pedal responses to protect the child from feeling undue stress. (Occasionally, the person who really needs a guidance talk may be the other staff member in the room!) If there is a danger of real harm, of course, the teacher does intervene. But if not, he or she might decide not to intervene at all, regarding the conflict as a learning experience and watching for a possible repeat of the behavior in the future.

Level Two: Socially Influenced Mistaken Behavior

Children at level two have not gotten to where they consistently trust their own viewpoints, skills, and developing values. They still have insecurities concerning safety needs. They tend to adjust their views and behaviors to accommodate those they perceive to have authority. This helps them fit in and feel a sense of belonging. So, for instance, they might follow the lead of a more powerful peer and join in calling another child "butt head." Or they might believe that an adult does not like another child whom she has embarrassed in front of the group for a mistaken behavior. Children at the level of socially influenced mistaken behavior might avoid or be unfriendly to this child, deferring to what they perceive is the teacher's attitude.

In the learning setting, children are susceptible to level two mistaken behavior both individually and in groups. Two illustrations of socially influenced mistaken behavior *as it affects individuals* follow.

From family members or neighborhood children, Lars has learned what we might call expletives, powerful words like sh*t that are written with asterisks in place of key letters. One day while Lars is constructing a building-set car, a wheel won't turn. Lars tries everything. Finally the child exclaims, "Sh*t, Teacher, I can't get this fr*cking wheel to work!"

Using a guidance talk, the teacher quietly teaches Lars alternative words that "don't bother people in school" and helps the child find a wheel that turns.

Rex, forty months old, is the third of five boys and comes from a home with a single parent. The parent lets the boys decide some matters on their own, like who decides what TV show to watch and who gets the extra dessert. Needless to say, roughhousing is a part of the decision making, a behavior Rex brings into the learning setting. The teachers have been working hard to establish a trust-based relationship with Rex. They have been teaching him ways to share and take turns that don't involve jumping on other kids.

Rex does not show deep-seated hostility in his problem solving through physicality, which indicates to the teachers that he is showing level two mistaken behavior (not level three). He simply has not yet learned how to get along with others in the learning setting. With firm but friendly teaching, including many guidance talks, Rex makes progress in using words with his mates. The arc of his progress is from physically taking, to saying "Gimme that," to asking "You done with that yet?" It has taken a few months, but Rex is showing considerably fewer physical conflicts, and the teachers—who worked hard at building relationships with him—are pleased.

Notice that the sources of the level two mistaken behaviors above were experiences outside the learning setting, experiences that taught the children lessons that they brought into the setting. Children also show socially influenced mistaken behavior as a result of immediate group dynamics within the learning setting, sometimes dramatically so. An illustration of socially influenced mistaken behavior that has gone public follows:

A new child was going to join the class, so, on the preceding day, the teacher had a group meeting and talked with the children about how the child had special needs and used a wheelchair and crutches to get around. She read them a book about a child in a wheelchair joining a program, hoping it would make Darla's transition easier. The next day, Darla, forty-two months old, wheeled herself into the dramatic play area. Chris and Jean, both fifty-three months old, started to enter the area. Chris said quietly to Jean, "I'm not playing with her. She's different." Jean said back to Chris, "Yeah, we're not playing with her. She's different." Other children in the vicinity heard the conversation. Quickly, teacher Rosetta asked the two to follow her to a quiet place nearby. She reminded them of the book and the discussion from the day before. Rosetta told them that everybody is different because everyone is their own person. She added, "In our group, we all play together and are good mates." She asked how the two could play with Darla. Chris said they could eat supper and went to join Darla. Jean didn't say anything and drifted off toward the blocks. Rosetta figured one child today, maybe both children tomorrow, and she made a note to talk with Jean later in the day.

The child who initiates socially influenced mistaken behavior often operates from level one experimentation mistaken behavior. The child does something or says something to control a situation that catches on with others. Chris was showing level one mistaken behavior here, influencing Jean to go along. Influenced by Chris, Jean was showing level two.

Teachers often hold group meetings both to prevent socially influenced mistaken behavior and to remedy it. Rosetta held the meeting the day before Darla joined in an effort to prevent the type of mistake that Chris and Jean fell into. She chose to have a guidance talk with the two as an intervention—made because there was a danger of psychological harm. When several children become (or might become) involved in an incident, an early childhood professional might lead a group meeting to resolve the issue. (See chapter 5 for more information on group meetings.)

Level Three: Survival (Strong Unmet Needs) Mistaken Behavior

Children at level three are experiencing toxic stress as a result of unmet safety needs. The source of this unmanageable stress might be challenging environmental experiences, atypical neurological development, or a combination of the two. (Note to readers: for level three mistaken behavior, I now use the term *survival mistaken behavior*, which is close to the term that Harlow originally used in 1975.)

Children at this third level perceive the world as threatening and themselves as victims in this threatening world. In a real sense, these children may be experiencing degrees of post-traumatic stress syndrome, due to witnessing or experiencing trauma (Lubit 2010).

Children at level three display mistaken attempts at survival behavior, misplaced efforts at protecting themselves from perceived threat. Cairone points out that, ironically, outside of the haven of the early learning setting, the survival behaviors may sometimes be a deterrent to the sources of threat and stress the children face (2016).

In the learning setting, these are children whose amygdala-driven behaviors result in extreme and repeated conflicts. They are vulnerable to being stigmatized because of their behavior and to falling into the stress-rejection cycle. These children are often the most difficult to like, but they are the most in need of an adult to be consistently friendly with them—outside of as well as during conflict situations.

What follow are types of level three mistaken (survival) behavior that these children show, each with an illustrative vignette.

"Freeze and Flee" Survival Behaviors Characteristic of Childhood Depression

- Rigid preference for behaviors and situations that are familiar, routine, and safe

- Inability or quiet refusal to engage in new experiences, which the child perceives as threatening

- Aloof and quietly rejecting reactions to friendly overtures from others

- Difficulty in building trust-based relationships

- Episodes of irritability or sadness out of balance with classroom events

 Mambe, thirty-eight months old, and his mother came to a rural town as refugees from eastern Africa. The mother got a job cleaning in a motel, and the owner helped the family get enrolled in a Head Start program. After entering the room on his second day, Mambe stood in a corner with tears in his eyes. The boy tried to open the door leading out, but it had a tricky latch. Marcy, the teacher, knelt down and quietly welcomed him. She brought him breakfast and put it on the end of the table; he ate by himself. Marcy said that Mambe looked like a deer in the headlights, so she took his hand and showed him the schedule. She explained when his mom would pick him up. Mambe's eyes wandered to where a child was rolling a ball down a V-shaped ramp. He watched for ten minutes but did not join. Later, after coming in from outside, Mambe got a ball and rolled it down the ramp. Another child picked it up. The teacher said, "Mambe, tell him it is your ball." "My ball!" said Mambe, and he took the ball back. At Marcy's suggestion, Mambe helped the other child find a ball, not saying a word, and went back to using the ramp.

Mistaken behavior is not always acting out. It is any behavior that indicates a child is hurting and doesn't know how else to act. As I see it, Marcy was doing a fine job here of helping Mambe, especially with DLS 1: gaining a sense of belonging in the group and acceptance as a little person of worth. This was a clear illustration of a growing proactive positive relationship at work.

"Fight" Survival Behaviors Related to Reactive Aggression

- Spontaneous aggression in disputes over valued objects

- Spontaneous aggression in disputes over territory infringement

- Spontaneous aggression in disputes over perceived privileges

- Mistrust of relationships, which adults must work to overcome

In the following, references are made to agressive behavior shown in relation to property, territory, and privlege. See pages 128–31 for further discussion of the role of these elements in children's conflicts.

 Harrison was twenty-seven months old when he joined the toddler room. After a few days, Harrison began to have conflicts just after arrival each morning. He would not wash his hands or come to the breakfast table. When teacher Rena tried to invite him, he worked himself into a rage, yelling the *F*-word (with his own particular pronunciation) and throwing things. Because his behavior distressed the other toddlers, Rena had to move him to a far corner of the room and hold him until he calmed down.

When Harrison repeated this behavior over the following days, Rena talked with Betty, his young mother, whom she had met only a few days earlier. Rena said she enjoyed having Harrison in her group. But, she told Betty, he was having a problem, especially after he arrived, and she wanted to help him. Betty shared that their house was small and the activities of some older family members often kept Harrison from settling down and getting to sleep. From their conversation, Rena concluded that the toddler's aggressive behavior might be due to lack of sleep related to conditions at home.

Rena worked out a strategy with Betty and the other staff members. When Harrison arrived in the morning, she approached him in a low-key way and gave him the choice of getting ready for breakfast or snuggling. Harrison usually chose snuggling and occasionally fell asleep. Throughout the day, Rena gave him choices between activities. Harrison began making choices and participating more. Rena and the two assistant teachers also sought out opportunities for one-on-one snuggling and *contact talks*—a few minutes of shared quality time—with him throughout each day.

Over that first month, Rena developed a relationship with Betty, who disclosed a bit more about the family's home situation. Rena learned that two male members of the family were particularly affected by poverty, showing mental health issues. This led Rena to refer the family to Early Head Start, where they could receive family assistance; however, there was a waiting list and therefore no opening for Harrison.

Sometimes Harrison ate breakfast. He tended to eat late and eat little, but at least he started eating. Gradually, Harrison accepted the toddler routine. Rena remained open to his need for a morning snuggle, but Harrison needed closeness on arrival only some days. The teachers realized that while they could not change Harrison's home environment, they could help him feel safe and welcome in the toddler room, and they could maintain a positive relationship with his mother.

"Fight" Survival Behaviors Related to Instrumental Aggression

- Aggressive strategies during disputes to gain valued objects

- Aggressive strategies during disputes to gain valued territory

- Aggressive strategies during disputes to gain valued privileges

Carlie, fifty-eight months old, had some serious issues with the adults in her program. One way she showed this strong emotion was by hiding behind the playhouse whenever it was time to go in. Almost daily, when an adult went to retrieve her, she grew defiant, leading to a dramatic conflict and sometimes a time-out in the room. On this day, Carlie got three other children to hide with her. When she saw the adult coming, she snuck past the children and the adult and got in line. She watched with a slight smile while the teacher herded the other three children back in line. The teacher mistakenly thanked Carlie for remembering to line up, relieved that on this day, it wasn't Carlie. (This mistaken behavior was level two for the other children, level three for Carlie.)

Carlie was using a strategy of *instrumental aggression* here, influencing others toward mistaken behaviors that were indirectly aggressive toward an adult. This is a sophisticated act of mistaken behavior, seen in the oldest, most worldly preschoolers. Suffice it to say that Carlie, no less than Mambe and Harrison, was experiencing trauma in her life. The staff was aware that her parents were in a divorce process, with the father being, in the words of the mother, "destructively domineering." Carlie was using amygdala-driven learning to attempt to control her unmanageable life and toxic stress. Instrumental aggression is perhaps the most challenging of behaviors shown by challenged children.

Safety Needs, Growth Needs, and the Democratic Life Skills

The five democratic life skills (DLS), first mentioned in the introduction, are a way of informally assessing and responding to where children are on the safety needs–growth needs continuum. Again, the five democratic life skills are as follows:

1. Finding acceptance as a member of the group and as a worthy individual

2. Expressing strong emotions in nonhurting ways

3. Solving problems creatively—independently and in cooperation with others

4. Accepting differing human qualities in others

5. Making decisions intelligently and ethically

The chief distinction in the construct is between the first two democratic life skills—which indicate the child is still attempting to meet needs for safety and a sense of belonging—and the second three, which indicate the child is working on needs for learning and psychological growth. Children tend to work on the skills in these two clusters rather than sequentially. By this I mean that there are connections between DLS 1 and 2, and teachers guide children toward gaining these abilities together.

As children meet basic needs, they gain in both the ability to feel acceptance and worth and to express strong emotions in nonhurting ways. At this point, in terms of brain development, children are switching from survival reactions driven by the amygdala system to more intentional responses governed by the brain's executive functions. They become able to respond to adult leadership that empowers progress on the growth needs, DLS 3, 4, and 5.

The difference is illustrated by a boy in child care whose older brother had just been arrested in front of him. Jason first expressed his unmanageable stress by losing control, especially at transition times, and by lashing out at others who he perceived were invading his personal space. Realizing the situation and its effects, staff worked on renewing their individual relationships with Jason and with maintaining close communication with Jason's family. Three weeks later, I was visiting the classroom and saw Jason working hard on an elaborate block structure. His teacher told me that Jason said he was building the jail "where I am going to see my brother after school." Progress here, I think, from DLS 1 and 2 to DLS 3—and the pathway to 4 and 5.

Children have their own styles of progress with DLS 3, 4, and 5, and show gains at different levels in regard to each skill. The fundamental point is that children working on the second three DLS have succeeded in meeting basic needs. The resulting sense of security allows them to work on the expression of mastery motivation, healthy executive functioning, and openness to new learning experiences and relationships. On this day, Jason was working by himself. On another day, he might be working with others.

The Democratic Life Skills and Levels of Mistaken Behavior

Children working on DLS 1 and 2 tend to show mistaken behavior at level three and sometimes level two. Children working on DLS 3, 4, and 5 tend to show mistaken behavior at level one and sometimes level two. Let us use the illustrations in this chapter to gain a sense of how the profiled children are doing in relation to the five skills—indicating where they are on the safety needs–growth needs continuum.

Ansha, fifty-six months, told Lena she was still getting used to Lena's blue buzz cut. Ansha was showing definite achievement in relation to solving a problem cooperatively (DLS 3), accepting a new difference in her friend (DLS 4), and making an intentional comment that took Lena's feelings into account (DLS 5). Ansha was not showing a mistaken behavior at all.

Jerome, forty-nine months, hit a child during the first week of the program and was put on a time-out chair. Jerome and his family had experienced the acute trauma of physical separation. Jerome had difficulty seeing he belonged in the program and was of worth (DLS 1). He clearly had difficulty expressing strong emotions in nonhurting ways (DLS 2). He was showing level three mistaken behavior.

Ryan, forty-one months, was carrying high stress around with him for largely neurological reasons. When he had to end an activity in which he was fully engaged, he panicked and fell to the floor screaming. He could have injured himself with this strong reaction, and he certainly startled those around him. For these reasons, Ryan was struggling with DLS 1 and 2. He was showing level three mistaken behavior.

Mambe, thirty-eight months, and his mother had experienced the extreme stress of persistent physical danger and persecution in their home country. This stress showed its effects in likely childhood depression—extreme survival freeze and flee tendencies. Mambe was just beginning to make gains with DLS 1 and was just beginning to work on DLS 2. His withdrawal was a level three mistaken behavior.

Harrison, twenty-seven months, brought unmanageable stress with him each morning for at least environmental reasons. The reactive aggression he showed by throwing chairs and lashing out at those around him was an anxiety attack. Harrison was struggling with DLS 1 and 2. He was showing level three mistaken behavior.

Carlie, fifty-eight months, showed the survival behavior of instrumental aggression. She roped three other children into hiding so as to intentionally fool the teacher, thus showing indirect aggression toward the teacher. The level three mistaken behavior was the child's attempt to control her general life circumstances that were out of control. Carlie was struggling with DLS 1 and DLS 2. Her mistaken behavior was at level three.

Cynthia, fifty-six months old, challenged herself by doing multiple puzzles at once. She was so engaged that she did not notice (or she ignored) that it was time to get ready and go outside. The lead teacher resolved the problem with Cynthia, realizing that she was showing a level one mistaken behavior. Cynthia was just beginning to work especially on DLS 3.

Amelia, forty-eight months old, decided to try a bit of mischief and tug on the hair of her sleeping neighbor. The teacher decided to ignore the level one mistaken behavior for the time being. In my view, Amelia was working on DLS 3, having not yet mastered the concept of solving problems cooperatively.

Amelia seemed to have a shy demeanor, which indicates she was working (in this instance somewhat humorously) on DLS 2.

You might have different ideas of where the children are in terms of the DLS and levels of mistaken behavior shown. That is fine. The constructs are intended to be used in a judgment-referenced and collaborative way to provide a guide for early childhood professionals as they seek to understand the behaviors of children in their groups. Perhaps these are the fundamental questions to ask: What is the overall stress level each child is dealing with, and how do I know?

Hopefully, the constructs explored here in chapter 1 can be of assistance as we turn to the next chapter. Chapter 2 begins our investigation of seven guidance practices designed to make stress manageable for each child in the group through proactive positive relationships and to teach conflict management skills that empower young children to solve their conflicts in nonhurting ways.

Discussion Questions

An element of being an early childhood professional is respecting the children, parents, and educators with whom you are working by keeping identities private. In completing follow-up activities, please respect the privacy of all concerned.

1. Reflect about a time when a teacher formed a proactive positive relationship with a child who was having a difficult time in the learning setting. Select an idea from the chapter that you believe helps explain the teacher's strategy in building the relationship.

2. Having read the chapter, what has changed about your understanding of the title phrase "challenging behaviors means challenged children"?

3. Think about a conflict in a group setting that for a child involved was either level one or level two mistaken behavior. What ideas from the chapter helped you make your assessment?

4. Think about a conflict in a group setting that for a child involved was level three mistaken behavior. What ideas from the chapter helped you make your assessment?

5. Which democratic life skills do you think the children in questions three and four have attained? Which are they still working on?

Key Concepts

Definitions of the Key Concepts can be found in the glossary on pages 177–84.

Attachment theory

Developmentally appropriate
practice

Executive functions

Experimentation mistaken
behavior

Instrumental aggression

Mastery motivation

Reactive aggression

Secure attachments

Socially influenced mistaken
behavior

Survival (strong unmet needs)
mistaken behavior

CHAPTER 2

Seven Guidance Practices

WHEN CONFLICTS HAPPEN, mistaken behavior occurs at any of the three levels. The range is from level one unintended mistaken behavior—a child thinks another child is done with a toy and tries to take it—to intentional level three mistaken behavior—the second child physically hurts the first child trying to take the toy.

The teacher's reaction to mistaken behavior—whether that of a technician using traditional discipline or a professional using guidance—affects whether children escalate and repeat mistaken behaviors or learn to resolve conflicts themselves.

Professionals not Technicians

In perhaps his most concise statement on progressive education, John Dewey characterized the role of the teacher this way: He said a teacher is not the guardian of some sanctified preset curriculum, rewarding some students and punishing others depending on their compliance in the duty of mastering it. Neither is the teacher one who sits back and simply watches in a child-centered learning system. Young learners cannot possibly know the path to a successful education on their own (Dewey 1997). For this reason, the teacher serves as friendly mediator between the logically structured curriculum and the psychologically learning child. In other words, in Dewey's terms, the teacher "psychologizes the curriculum," guiding the learner to find personal meaning through learning experiences via the curriculum, thus nurturing the child's intrinsic mastery motivation.

A guidance professional is open to learning, even as she or he teaches, and is ever responsive to the individual child, even while building a setting encouraging

Thanks to *Exchange Magazine* for permission to adapt my article in the November–December 2015 issue for this chapter.

for all children. In contrast, an adult who performs the job as a technician works to establish routines in program and schedule and makes it a priority for children to follow those routines.

The following illustrates differences between the mind-set of an adult who is a technician and one who is a guidance professional.

It is Julio's first day in the group. As a forty-eight-month-old, he and his family are new to the community. At home Julio often builds with Legos he inherited from an older sibling. He sees a box of Legos at a table. In the free time before group, he quietly begins building. The call for large group is made. The teacher is getting other children into the circle and does not notice that Julio keeps working.

A technician's reaction might well be this: Ready to begin, the adult spots Julio still at the table. Not getting up, she uses a commanding voice across the room, "Come to circle now, young man. In my classroom we do things in certain ways and every child does them!" Julio gets up from the table, looking scared, and walks to the group.

A guidance professional's response would be this: Ready to begin, the adult spots Julio still at the table. Smiling, she gets up and walks over to him. She kneels down and speaks quietly to him, "Julio, this is your first day, and it is our job to help you learn our schedule. It is group time now, so come sit by me, so we can help you get to know the other children." Still smiling, she stands up, takes Julio's hand, and the two walk over to the group.

The illustration is loaded, to be sure, but let me ask you: Have you had some teachers who were more like the adult in the first scenario? More like the adult in the second? What difference did the teacher's mind-set make to you during the time you were with that adult?

Dewey (1997) wrote that when classrooms become active laboratories with children engaging cooperatively in learning experiences, our whole concept of discipline changes. Managing behavior becomes a process performed as a responsive leader, not as a dictatorial boss. In our terms, this means that as leaders, adults work as professionals, not technicians. They continuously make judgments about situations and work to resolve problems in ways that teach rather than punish.

Of course, being a guidance professional does not always go this smoothly— sometimes our hypotheses and responses in conflict situations are only partially successful. Like all of us, guidance professionals are more humanoid than angelic, but they strive to act on behalf of our better angels, learning from experiences—as we ask children to do—to resolve matters more successfully next time. We learn even as we teach.

Seven Guidance Practices

Seven guidance practices empower the work of the early childhood professional; each is introduced here and discussed in more depth in chapters to follow. Many of the practices are also topics of the Guidance Matters columns in *Young Children* written between 2005 and 2014 (an annotated list and downloading information can be found under "Resources by Dan Gartrell" in the appendix). Readers should note that the seven practices all depend on the teacher's taking time to build positive, proactive relationships with every child in the group.

1. An Encouraging Early Childhood Community for Every Child

Some teacher-technicians think that if most children in the group are getting along and doing well, that is good enough. Yet a setting is only truly developmentally appropriate if every child is successful (Hyson and Biggar Tomlinson 2014). It is the other few children who, due to temperament and behavior, tend to rub the teacher the wrong way. Adults can have personality conflicts even with preschoolers, but teachers who use guidance find a way to manage their feelings in relation to individual children. They use their emotional-social intelligence and experience to build a positive relationship with every child—for the good of the challenged children, the rest of the group, and the adults involved.

For me, an encouraging learning community is a place where every child wants to be, even when they are sick—as opposed to a place where children do not want to be when they are well. The teacher uses two fundamental practices to enable every child to feel welcome and valued.

First, the early childhood professional monitors and modifies the program to make sure it is developmentally appropriate for every child. Often young children are just too energetic for a traditional preschool day that has teacher-directed large groups, follow-directions craft activities (instead of open-ended art), limited choices in the use of materials and centers, and lots of sit-down pencil-and-paper lessons (Martin and Slack 2015). When teachers modify the program to include stable small groups that do things together, many open-ended, hands-on activity choices, and a lot of active-play experiences—both outdoors and in activity rooms—more children can get engaged and feel included (Copple and Bredekamp 2009).

Second, the early childhood professional uses relationship-building techniques like personal acknowledgment, taking the time to compliment details in a child's efforts and achievements—not saying, "good job," for example, but rather, "You used lots of colors in your picture." The adult uses such occasions to move to a second technique: *contact talk*. Contact talk is quality time spent with an individual child. The adult listens and follows the child's line of conversation. Not meant to preach, screech, or teach, contact talks are intended to allow the adult and child to get to know each other and to build mutual trust—the foundation of a positive relationship.

To begin contact talks, the adult frequently gives positive acknowledgment to what the child is doing:

TEACHER: You are working hard on that firehouse, Willis. You've used almost all of the blocks!

The truthful compliment tends to lead into a friendly conversation and the opportunity for the adult to positively acknowledge what the child may be thinking and feeling. Pausing after the compliment, the child usually continues the conversation:

WILLIS: Yeah, my auntie fights fires and she rides on the truck. I got to get on it at the firehouse.

TEACHER: You must be proud of your auntie.

WILLIS: Yep, Auntie Jackie is the best. She showed me all over the place.

Whatever name these conversations are given—powerful interactions, contact talks, etc.—regular shared positive moments between the child and adult do what nothing else can to build positive, proactive relationships. Pausing to give the child a chance to decide how to respond really helps. The teacher is affirming the worth of the child to the child by giving the brief gift of time.

Chia, aged thirty-eight months, has covered her blue paper with white chalk.

Her teacher says, "You are working hard on your picture and have used a lot of white." Chia looks at the picture and replies, "Yep, diz is a bizzard and my dad's back there plowin', but you can't see him." Teacher, smiling, says, "Your dad must have a pretty big plow." Chia describes the plow in detail, and the two enjoy the moment together.

Occasionally a child will not respond to a teacher's positive acknowledgment. The teacher keeps the quality time going by maintaining a friendly physical presence. In this case, the contact talk was only a little verbal and more nonverbal. This is good enough. Contact talks don't have to be lengthy, but they do need to be regular, with every child every day. We explore these matters more in chapter 3.

2. Working with Families on Behalf of the Child

Parents are the first and foremost teachers of their children. Teachers only help. But being a parent is a difficult job, made more so if one is alone, if expenses outpace income, if family members have mental health and dependency issues, if children have extreme temperaments, if the family's culture is different from the community's, and especially if surrogate parents are raising the child. In such cases, the help that early childhood professionals provide is crucial. At no other level of education can teachers make such a profound difference in the life of a child as when they are friendly to a family in need.

The early childhood professional works with warm persistence to build relationships with family members. Recognizing that modern family life is complicated, the teacher learns as much as possible about each family, works to build mutual trust, and helps family members build on their strengths for the good of the child.

Maria's mom, Priscilla, did not attend the teacher's greeting meeting and first conference. She did not return phone messages that the teacher left. Fighting the notion that this parent doesn't care, teacher Inez talked with other staff members. She learned that Priscilla worked as a cocktail waitress from two to eleven p.m. and that the children stayed with Grandma while she worked. Inez called Priscilla at the restaurant, said how much she enjoyed having Maria in her group, and asked if the two could meet sometime in a booth on Priscilla's break! Reluctantly, Priscilla asked the manager, and he gave his permission. Priscilla and Inez met a few times during the fall and got along well. Inez saw how well when Priscilla accepted her invitation and began coming to the classroom to read to the children before her shift.

With the teacher's leadership, Priscilla progressed from simply receiving and accepting program information to becoming an active participant in ways that benefited the entire program. The teacher was key here. Inez overcame a stereotype that might have kept Priscilla distant from the program. She realized that when working with families, the teacher needs to be friendly first and stay with it for the long haul in the effort to empower family engagement. By her efforts, Inez was able to convey to Priscilla that they were teammates on the same team and could work together.

In chapter 4, we look at a construct of four levels of family engagement within the early childhood community. As we will explain, Priscilla progressed not just to engagement at level one (receiving information), but to level three (benefiting the entire program)—great progress easily determined when we study the four levels in that chapter.

3. Group Meetings

Group meetings begin where circle times leave off, going beyond the routines of weather and weekly calendar. Group meetings bring the events of the day, along with problems, experiences, and individual activity planning, into thoughtful discussion. They involve respectful talking and listening that encourages the group to share and solve problems together.

Teachers might introduce an activity: "Today in the art area, you are going to make your own special outdoors pictures. Who can think of something you like to do outdoors?" Or they might lead a discussion about a problem in the classroom that has gone public:

 "Yesterday some children were saying words that bother other children and teachers. The words were *butt head*." (Pauses for giggling and guilty looks.) "Could someone share how you would feel if someone said that to you?" The adult then guides the group in polite discussion of how this problem can be solved. In line with an established guideline, the names of individual children are not used. The teacher follows up privately with children that she or he knows have been using the words.

Group meetings do much to build encouraging early childhood communities. They are versatile in that they can address both everyday matters and public problems within the group. You may wonder whether group meetings can work with preschoolers or even with toddlers. I know of toddler settings where the adults hold group meetings every day. A classic anecdote about a group meeting in a toddler group is provided in chapter 5. Teaser: the topic of the group meeting is biting.

Group meetings are a valuable lead-up activity for living and participating in a democracy—think caucuses here—with the teacher serving as leader. They are like early childhood town meetings that teach children and adults alike that the early childhood community is inclusive of all. They encourage all members to know that they belong and can participate successfully in the group.

4. During Conflicts, Calm All First

Traditionally, teacher-technicians react to dramatic conflicts by restoring order—they comfort the victim and punish the perpetrator(s). Though the adults may have restored order for a while, they have done little to help the parties learn how to reconcile after a conflict and learn how to resolve matters in a more peaceable manner next time.

In contrast, after triaging for physical harm, early childhood professionals first calm all involved, beginning with themselves. If any of the children are very upset, the teacher may remove them from the situation. But this action is different than forcing a time-out—placing a child on a chair *as a consequence* of something the child has done. No one can resolve a conflict when emotions are high. A teacher removes children to help them calm down. Then the teacher uses a *guidance talk* or *conflict mediation* (to follow) to model and teach reconciliation and management skills for next time.

Often, separation for a cooling-down time is unnecessary. The teacher might have the children take deep breaths and otherwise ensure that they really are calm before helping them mediate the situation. Still, if a child *has* totally lost control and there is an imminent danger of harm, the adult may need to use the calming technique of last resort, the *passive bear hug* (see "On Restraining to Prevent Harm" on pp. 116–19 for more information).

Calming children before trying to help them learn to effectively manage conflicts is a crucial guidance step. Chapter 6 explores the important matter of calming everyone down (including yourself) as well as other crisis de-escalation techniques for the teacher that are part of the guidance approach.

5. Guidance Talks

Building on positive relationships with children in the group, the guidance talk is the intervention of choice when a child is involved in a strong conflict, whether with a peer or an adult. As with class meetings and conflict mediation, the purpose of the guidance talk is to resolve the conflict peaceably and teach the child what he or she can learn at the time about nonhurting responses to use in future conflict situations. A primary consideration is to avoid embarrassing the child, perhaps the most common form of punishment used in early childhood settings.

The adult first gets calm and helps the child cool down, sometimes by moving to a quieter place in the room. After the child is calm enough, the adult works with the child to determine exactly what happened, giving respect to the child's viewpoint. They then discuss how they can make the situation better and what the child could do next time instead of showing aggression. Note that at the close of the guidance talk, the adult does not force an apology, but instead asks how the child can help the other person feel better. If needed, the adult gives the child time to think of a way.

Bernard, forty-six months old, is playing house with Carla and Dominic, both fifty-two months old. They are pretending that packing nuggets are mac and cheese. Bernard, who is not as far along in his development as the other children, asks for more. Carla shows him the empty bowl and says there are no more. Bernard gets upset and sweeps all the plates off the table. He then gets under the table and pouts. The other two get out of the way and watch. Teacher Basma sits on the floor by Bernard and rubs his back to help him calm down. The two quietly talk about what happened and why. A few minutes later, Bernard climbs out and starts putting the pretend mac and cheese back in the bowl. Carla and Dominic help. At the teacher's quiet prompt, Bernard says, "Thank you." Basma correctly infers that this is Bernard's apology. With the teacher watching, the three continue their lunch; no one worries that the "food" had been on the floor.

The guidance talk is the macaroni and cheese of guidance practices. It is an individual talk between a teacher and child, with the adult kneeling or sitting at the child's level and perhaps making friendly physical contact. The adult avoids public embarrassment and moral judgments about the conflict or the child. She or he engages the child in a problem-solving process, informally following the five steps used in conflict mediation (listed under the next heading). Being pure guidance, the purpose of the guidance talk is not to punish a child for making a mistake in judgment, but to help the child learn as much as possible about reconciliation and how to manage similar problems in a more civil way in the future. Positive follow-up with the child after the guidance talk is always a good idea. We explore guidance talks as a staple of guidance practice in chapter 7.

6. Conflict Mediation

Conflict mediation happens when an outside party guides parties in a conflict to civilly resolve it. In early childhood settings, the two or three parties experiencing the conflict have just begun developing emotion management skills. Teachers who use conflict mediation have taken a key step in adopting guidance as an approach. They recognize that in an environment that is encouraging for all, even preschool children can make great progress with managing emotions and resolving conflicts civilly—abilities that we work on for our entire lives.

Conflict mediation offers learning opportunities for both participants and onlookers beyond the actual resolution of the conflict. Key language skills, social studies skills, sometimes even math skills are modeled and taught through the process. In the words of one teacher, "Conflict mediation is not a distraction from our program; it is a vital part of our program."

Our illustration of conflict mediation at work is a sixty-month-old mediating between a fifty-two-month-old and a forty-one-month-old. We use this wonderful illustration to make the point that the mediator does not have to have a master's degree to make this practice work and, in fact, does not even have to be an adult!

 When Beth began as a teacher in the child care center, Jeremiah, aged thirty-nine months, showed behaviors that indicated he had clearly been used to sitting on the dreaded green chair. In contrast, Beth used a mediation system for handling conflicts that actively involved the children. Two years later, a few weeks before he was to start kindergarten, Jeremiah saw Curt, fifty-two months old, trying to get Amy, forty-one months old, to give up a truck. Beth watched in amazement as Jeremiah walked over to the two and said, "What's going on, guys?" Curt said it was time for Amy to give the truck to him. Jeremiah asked Amy if she was done. Amy clutched the truck, turned away, and shook her head. Jeremiah told Curt, "I don't think Amy is done yet. Use another, okay?" Curt nodded. Jeremiah walked away showing a confident smile that Beth had never seen before. Amy played with the truck a bit more and then gave it to Curt.

For years I have been recommending a five-step practice, the *five-finger formula*, for teachers to use during conflict mediation:

1. Cool everyone down, starting with yourself.

2. Use negotiation to get the children to agree how each saw the conflict.

3. Help the children brainstorm solutions to the conflict.

4. Agree on a solution and try it.

5. Monitor and follow up.

For some reason, Jeremiah had not read the material on the five-finger formula, but he used the basics well enough to get the conflict resolved. This is a main point in the use of conflict mediation: like other guidance practices, perfection is not needed to make the practice work. We take a good look at using conflict mediation with preschoolers and even toddlers in chapter 8.

7. Comprehensive Guidance

When children cause conflicts that are serious and repeated, early childhood professionals need to bring a mix of guidance practices together in a coordinated plan. The teacher holds a meeting with all staff members who work with the child. This is not a gripe session; the team tries to understand the child's pattern of behavior. The lead adult then contacts family members, using the urgency of the situation to request a meeting.

At the meeting, after starting with positives about the child, the lead puts the problem the child is having in the context of overall progress the staff sees. The staff and parents discuss the need for a formal or informal individual guidance plan (IGP) for improvement in the area identified. They work out a plan together with the family. The staff gives encouragement to the family to work on the plan at home. They monitor progress in relation to the plan and hold one or more follow-up meetings with the parents.

Too many early childhood programs across the nation have a history of expelling children who show serious and repeated conflicts. In the guidance approach, removing children as a result of their behavior is a last resort, only after an IGP is developed, tried, modified, and tried again. Building relations with parents from the very first day is essential should an IGP later prove necessary. In making the case that an IGP meeting is necessary, staff members may have to say that this is the only way the child can continue in the program. But hopefully, establishing positive relations from the beginning will make this move unnecessary. (An IGP planning sheet can be found in the appendix and is available for download at http://dangartrell.net/presentation-handouts.)

The more serious the situation, the more the early childhood professional involves and collaborates with other adults to find solutions. Good relationships among adult professionals are as important as good relationships with children and families. Friendly communication, even if sometimes firm, is always at the heart of guidance.

Collaborate: Plan Together, Work Together

There is an unfortunate tradition in American education that goes back to one-room schools in our nation's past (Gartrell 2014). It is that the individual teacher handles all situations alone. We see this widespread practice in the mass-class phenomenon in K–12 public schools: One teacher and twenty students or more. In class sizes too large, the teacher handles all situations up to a breaking point, when the student must be temporarily removed. At that point, there is a mark not only against the student, but also against the teacher, who could not handle the situation without temporary expulsion.

By using differentiated staffing, even in group-family child care programs, early childhood education leads the way, modeling a system that alleviates the mass-class phenomenon. In encouraging learning communities, the model is two or more adults in a more reasonably sized group. One adult is a lead teacher and the others are assistants, who nonetheless lead small groups and build proactive positive relationships with individual children (Gartrell 2014). When problems arise in the learning setting, the *teaching team* pulls together and addresses the matter in a collaborative way.

The golden rule of *collaboration* is that early childhood professionals accomplish together what they cannot alone. But as with other aspects of guidance, the teamwork happens because the lead teacher builds the team from day one. Saying no to a traditional professional/nonprofessional separation of roles, lead teachers assign groups to assistants who become primary care providers for those groups. Leads treat team members with appreciation, building mutual appreciation in the process (The Greta Horwitz Center 2016).

So, if a lead teacher sees a spill, she or he cleans it up. If an assistant has a penchant for music or science activities, the assistant is able to use and grow those skills. If an assistant works well with a child who has frequent conflicts, the teacher assigns the assistant leadership tasks with the child and often assigns the child to the assistant's group. The children in the encouraging community, as well as other adults, benefit from experiencing this collaborative (hence democratic) rather than authoritarian staffing system. Moreover, young children in such settings do not have to begin mass-class public education until they have more experience and brain development.

When comprehensive guidance becomes necessary, the lead teacher is always the captain of the team but expects and encourages the team to work together—on behalf of the child and the encouraging community. The teaching-team model is not automatic; it requires perspective taking and interactive scaffolding taught and modeled by the lead teacher. Especially during challenging times, this leadership needs to be firm and friendly. The more serious the conflicts a child is experiencing, the more the teaching team needs to work together. When circumstances warrant, the lead professional expands the team to include family members, other professionals in the program, and sometimes professionals from outside agencies. Working together, caring adults can accomplish what they cannot—and should not be expected to—accomplish alone.

Discussion Questions

An element of being an early childhood professional is respecting the children, parents, and educators with whom you are working by keeping identities private. In completing follow-up activities, please respect the privacy of all concerned.

1. Which of the seven guidance practices have you seen used with effectiveness by a caring early childhood professional? Protecting privacy of all parties, share an illustration and tell why you think it is an effective example of good guidance.

2. Which of the seven guidance practices do you feel *most comfortable* with yourself? Which have you used or seen used in ways that seem to work on a regular basis?

3. Which of the seven guidance practices seems the *most challenging* for you to move toward and use as a teacher? Share your thoughts about why and how (or whether) you might make a start at using the practice.

Key Concepts

Definitions of the Key Concepts can be found in the glossary on pages 177–84.

Collaboration	Group meetings
Conflict mediation	Guidance talk
Contact talk	Passive bear hug
Five-finger formula for conflict mediation	Teaching team

CHAPTER 3

An Encouraging Learning Community for Every Child

ROREY, TWENTY-NINE MONTHS OLD, IS USUALLY a kid on the go in her child care program. But she missed Wednesday, Thursday, and Friday with an ear infection. The family physician put Rorey on an antibiotic and told Brooke, Rorey's mom, that Rorey could go back to child care when she felt better. On Monday, Rorey decided she was feeling up to it. Brooke was going to have Rorey stay with her dear grandpa one more day, but Rorey insisted, "Go see Dacia."

As she brought Rorey into child care, Brooke was apologetic. Smiling, Dacia said, "We get that a lot. We'll watch Rorey and make sure she doesn't get too tired. Feel free to call and check up on her." As Brooke and Dacia discussed the matter, Rorey had already gotten busy at the playdough table.

An *encouraging learning community* is a place where children want to go even when they are sick, as distinct from a place where children don't want to go even when they are well! An encouraging community begins in the mind of the early childhood professional. To create a welcoming community in which all feel included and fully able to learn, the adult practices all guidance, all the time.

Here are five characteristics of the effective early learning community, which this chapter explores. The EELC

One: is relationship rich,

Two: accepts that young children learn through their bodies,

Three: moves beyond rules to guidelines,

Four: fosters creativity, and

Five: is culturally competent.

Characteristic One: Is Relationship Rich

We talked earlier about the importance of early childhood professionals having proactive positive relationships with the children in their groups. As mediator between the logical curriculum and the psychological child, the teacher uses positive acknowledgment (specific compliments) and contact talks to build trust and reinforce a sense of safety and belonging in the child (democratic life skill one). For all children in the group, the early childhood professional works to sustain DLS 1 and 2 as the foundation for empowering movement to the growth-related democratic life skills.

Even when young children become involved in conflicts, the adult uses guidance practices that, while firm, still support positive relationships. Teachers remain firm with the guidance basic that no harm should be done, but they are firm and friendly in teaching to this principle, not firm and harsh (Watson 2003).

Recognizing that the natural social group for the young child is the family, the adult works to replicate this grouping style in care and education settings. For me, this means using *family groups* as a basic organizational pattern—stable groups of a small number of often multiaged children doing things together with the same primary care adult. Some of these adults may not have a teaching certification, but they work with a lead teacher who does. Part of the criteria for setting up family groups is determining which adult relates well with which children. One does not need to have a degree to build a proactive positive relationship with a child and to lead a small group.

Guidance professionals recognize that young children and large groups are not a natural match. Brief interactive (often musical) and active large groups have a valuable place in the program, as do interactive group meetings. Done well, they help build group spirit. But many activities that technicians assume are essentials in large groups—weather, calendar, flannel board stories, ritual book reading, sharing an interesting object by passing it around the circle—are better done in family groups. If teachers at the next level insist on extended full-group activities, the children will be another year older, and most will adjust with less difficulty.

Teacher Myra found an old classic in the public library, *I Am a Bunny*. She was reading the book to her family group of seven before lunch. On one page, Nicolas the Bunny is lying in a field of detailed vegetation, looking up at a sky of clouds.

A child points to a tiny wild strawberry at the bottom of the page. Sam says, "Look at that berry." "Yes," Myra says, "that is a strawberry." "I know," Sam replies. "My dad and me was picking berries. My dad put his nose down to smell the flower and a bee came and stung him on the nose!" (Ouch!)

The children and Myra all shared bee stories. Eventually they got back to the book. Myra felt really good about the conversation. The children were practicing language skills that included speaking and listening, vocabulary building, and sequencing and comprehension, not to mention meaningful nature concepts (including the value of bees). She realized this conversation and subsequent learning would have been difficult to achieve in the full group of eighteen children. In her family group, the book came alive for the children in a way she could not have anticipated.

Characteristic Two: Accepts That Young Children Learn through Their Bodies

Young children learn through their bodies, from the exploration of big body movement to the experimentation of eye-hand coordination to practice with tools and materials. Restriction of movement, such as through an overemphasis on prescribed cutting, coloring and pasting, and passive sit-down activities, is unnatural for young children. As young mammals, children are by nature active; they need to move to learn.

Many preschool teachers have been influenced to conclude that their job is to socialize young children to the sit-down/follow-directions classrooms that were inevitably to come. Growing agreement in the field challenges this traditional view (Copple and Bredekamp 2009; Martin and Slack 2015; Sanders 2002). Fighting to control young children's natural impulse to get up and move has led to too many me-against-you classroom scenarios. Though a few children can perhaps conform to this developmentally inappropriate expectation, many more cannot. Besides, as the saying goes, "sitting is the new smoking"—think inactive lifestyles here—including for children.

Boys and girls alike suffer in mind-over-body classrooms (Martin and Slack 2015)—though boys seem to suffer more. Some teacher-technicians even have a term for the short attention spans, restlessness, rambunctiousness, and rowdy behavior they see in boys who are not ready for their programs. They call it "boy behavior," which is really a discreet criticism of the natural need to move and be active felt 24/7 by many boys. These adults do not recognize that children (girls and boys) who show these mistaken behaviors are reacting in developmentally appropriate ways to developmentally *inappropriate* expectations (Gartrell 2012). The mistaken behaviors are in fact caused by inappropriate practices that teacher-technicians feel they are supposed to use: program-caused mistaken behavior.

The following is from Dan and Kathleen Sonsteng's March 2008 Guidance Matters column in Young Children. *Thanks to NAEYC for permission to use this material.*

Five-year-old Jacob attends the preschool where I (Jackie) am student teaching. Jacob often instigates rough-and-tumble play with his mates, which sometimes gets him and them in trouble. One day during outdoor time, Jacob wanted to play catch with a foam football. Even though I am not athletic, I took the opportunity, hoping for a one-on-one conversation.

Jacob: Jackie, do you want to play catch with me?

Jackie: Sure, I would love to play catch with you. (*We start tossing the ball.*) You like to play catch.

Jacob: I play with my dad all the time. He is really good. (*Jacob throws a really nice spiral.*)

Jackie: Wow! That was a nice throw. How did you do that?

Jacob: You put your fingers across the laces.

(*Jacob comes over and shows me where to place my fingers on the ball.*)

Jacob: You do it like this. Then you throw the ball. My dad taught me how to throw like that. That is how the quarterbacks throw the ball. (*Jacob tosses the ball really hard at me.*)

Jackie: Hey, you threw that really hard!

JACOB: Yeah, I did. I work out my muscles. I do push-ups like this (*shows me the arm movements*) and I do these things (*does an impression of a sit-up*). My dad does them too. He does them all the time.

JACKIE: So, Jacob, what else do you like to play?

JACOB: I play football, baseball, soccer, and basketball.

(*I wait for him to talk again.*)

JACOB: I like to play games. I like to play checkers. It's a game where you have little round disks, and they are red and black. You go and jump over other people and take their pieces away from them. (*He jumps to illustrate.*)

(*We continue playing catch for a while.*)

JACOB: Do you want to sit down and play catch?

JACKIE: Sure, if you want to. (*I sit on the bench while Jacob remains standing a few feet away. We start to play catch again, now more gently.*)

TEACHER EMILY: Okay, everyone, time to go inside!

Jackie was learning here what early childhood educators increasingly recognize: healthy child development—including brain development—relies on physical activity. From enjoyment in using movement skills to blood circulation that builds brains and bodies, and from obesity prevention to concept formation, the benefits of physical activity make it a must in the daily schedule. When Jacob described playing checkers and suggested that Jackie might want to sit down, he showed cognitive, linguistic, and even emotional-social learning—complete with a whole-body demonstration of jumping pieces in checkers!

Because Jackie ventured outside her comfort zone in joining Jacob in the physical activity, she made this situation richly educational—for herself and for Jacob. Through their shared experience, Jackie got to know Jacob better. In the future, she can talk with the teacher and use games and increased physical activity to help Jacob and his buddies become more consistently engaged in the daily program.

Accommodates Vigorous Activity

Some teachers worry that vigorous activity, if permitted, will degenerate into aggressive play and someone will be hurt (Carlson 2011). Many teachers have witnessed the *superhero phenomenon* in which children assume the role of make-believe heroes and become overly aggressive. Problems can be reduced, however, by using class meetings to define and set limits for rough-and-tumble play.

After a class meeting about using friendly touches only, a teacher found the discussion helpful on the playground. He came upon a World Wrestling Federation–style match of four boys, one of whom was yelling while being sat on! The teacher reminded the boys what friendly touches meant, and with his help, the boys decided to wrestle invisible space invaders instead. The four got bored with the make-believe wrestling and soon became first responders—still big body play, but without the aggressive undertones.

Two practices can assist teachers in maintaining a balance between addressing children's need for rough-and-tumble play and limiting aggression during this play. First, make guidelines with the children that clearly ensure everyone's safety. Second, promote imaginative and creative play to move beyond "narrowly scripted play that focuses on violent actions" (Levin 2003, 62). The teacher in the above example used both of these practices.

Because young children are "active critters" (as a classroom volunteer once commented) we know that including vigorous play in the learning program is essential. A teacher with a particularly active group of eighteen children, including fourteen boys, took the following steps:

- She moved all of the furniture three feet in from the walls and put a strip of colored duct tape around the perimeter. The teacher held a class meeting to introduce the new walking track, which was open during morning choice time. The walking track was used daily, especially by a few children. After guideline reminders that it was for walking exercise and not for running, it became an often-used part of the environment.

- She set up a physical fitness center next to the housekeeping area. In an introductory class meeting, the teachers established that both girls and boys would be using the center. It included a weight table and stationary bike bought at a garage sale; weights made from a shortened broom handle and two half-gallon plastic jugs with wax in them; a balance beam; and a mini-tramp that the children had to pass a competency test on (!) in order to use. The physical fitness center was open during choice times. Boys and girls visited the center often, including a group of fitness buff regulars.

- Besides modifying the room to accommodate her active group, the teacher took the children either outside or to the active-play room right away every morning. No one else was using these facilities at this time, and she found that this schedule change really helped get muscles moving and blood flowing—including her own. Teacher Lynnea made a point of joining in with the children (as Jackie did above) and joked that her new program became her way to stay in shape! (Not a bad idea, eh?) She noted that when some particularly active children returned to the classroom for choice time, they went right to the mini-tramp for more vigorous play! She also noted that the group became more intentionally busy and less restless after these program changes (King 2012).

In this day and age, we can acknowledge Lynnea's program as a valid part of the growing, national anti–childhood obesity movement (search the President's Council on Physical Fitness, Sports, and Nutrition; National Association for Sport and Physical Education). For so many reasons, physically active early childhood programs are crucial to the healthy development of the whole child.

Characteristic Three: Moves beyond Rules to Guidelines

Think about likely differences in the learning climates in these settings:

- One preschool group at the end of a hall has the rule "No talking in line." Another has the guideline "We are quiet in line so we don't bother others."

- One *kindergarten* classroom has the rule "Don't hand in work with mistakes." Another has the guideline "Mistakes are okay. We just need to learn from them."

In a *Young Children* article worth revisiting, Wien (2004) makes the case that rules tend not to be helpful in early childhood communities. Rules are usually stated as negatives. In fact, the way most rules are worded, it seems as if adults expect children to break them (Wien 2004). For example, with a "No hitting" rule, teachers often feel pressure to be hypervigilant for this behavior. Then they can only ignore the behavior or punish the child when it happens—limited options indeed. Even when rules are not totally negative, such as "Be nice to your friends," they may have an unspoken "or else" implication in teachers' minds.

When an adult enforces rules with children, the children know they have done something wrong. However, the negative experience in rule enforcement does not teach them what to do instead (Readdick and Chapman 2000), as seen when an adult says, "You know the rule. No hitting! Go to the time-out chair." Busy with comforting the victim and punishing the perpetrator, adults easily forget the importance of teaching children positive strategies, like using words or getting a teacher, as alternatives to hitting—or being hit by—a classmate.

Rules too easily reduce teaching to a priority on enforcement. A rule-enforcement orientation can make teachers stricter than they really want to be. Rules can cause teachers to mentally label children, lump them into groups, and enforce rules accordingly. They find themselves being lenient with the children who mostly obey rules, those they have labeled as good, and being strict with the children who often break rules, those they have labeled as naughty. Remember that a time-out is really a temporary expulsion from the group, an embarrassing punishment (Readdick and Chapman 2000). Studies show that children frequently subjected to punitive rule enforcement feel rejected, develop negative self-images, and may have long-term problems with aggressiveness in school and life (Ladd 2008; Ettekal and Ladd 2015). These kids too easily fall into the stress-rejection cycle.

Moving to Guidelines

The purpose of having guidelines is to teach children to use them. For instance, with the guideline "We are friendly with our mates," the adult can calm down an upset child, then teach the child how to use friendlier words to express her feelings. (This teaching is built on a positive adult-child relationship that the adult is always working to improve [Watson 2003].) In this sense, guidelines are not just permissive rules—a common misconception. When there is danger of harm, teachers are firm in the use of guidelines—just firm and friendly.

In teaching guidelines, practices like guidance talks and conflict mediation work well, along with group meetings. The expectation is that children live up to guidelines all the time, not just sometimes. Guidelines identify positive expectations that teachers help children (and sometimes other adults in the classroom) learn and use.

When adults model these positive expectations, they teach children the skills they need for civil living (Copple and Bredekamp 2009). From the guideline "We are friendly with our mates," a child extrapolates, saying, "Please share the markers." Perhaps with a teacher looking on, the comment invites dialogue and problem resolution. This set of interactions sure beats demanding, refusing, grabbing, pushing away, and the teacher's enforcing a "No fighting" rule.

With infants and toddlers, guidelines are expectations in teachers' minds. Teachers consistently refer to and model them in teaching prosocial behaviors. An example is saying, "Friendly touches, Freddie," as the teacher helps Freddie give gentle pats to another child.

With older preschoolers, writing and posting guidelines (with the children) provides a functional literacy activity as well as a quick visual reminder. Here are four example guidelines, with perhaps fewer used in preschool and four or five in kindergarten and the elementary grades. (Too many at any level makes things complicated.)

- We are friendly to others and ourselves.

- We solve problems together.

- We listen to each other.

- Mistakes are okay. We just need to learn from them.

One Head Start classroom had only one guideline: "We are friendly with our mates." (These teachers preferred the term *mates*, as in classmates, to *friends*. They respected the children's right to define their own friendships.)

Moving to the positive requires an attitude shift by the teacher from being a technician to being a professional. A technician operates with the ongoing mission of rule enforcement. In contrast, a teacher who is a professional continuously makes judgments about situations based on a mission to understand and guide—a mission greatly aided by the use of guidelines that transcend rules and their baggage.

In the process of becoming more effective professionals, teachers need to trust in and refine their own developing skills of observation, communication, and relationship building. Change, which often takes some courage, begins in the mind of the teacher. Adults learn even as they teach, and that is a good thing—for the children and for the adults in the encouraging learning community.

The previous section is adapted from my January 2012 Guidance Matters column in *Young Children*. Thanks to NAEYC for permission to use this material.

Characteristic Four: Fosters Creativity

In the second half of the twentieth century, a number of wise psychologists wrote about human development in ways that predicted recent neurological research findings on the effects of stress and stress management in individuals' lives. Abraham Maslow and Carl Rogers were two of these psychologists, and a third was Erik Erikson. Erikson (1963) is known for his construct of eight fundamental life challenges that individuals experience across the lifespan, infancy through old age. The first four challenges, occurring during childhood, indicate the importance of relationships that are supportive of a child's physical and psychological needs. With good enough parenting (it doesn't have to be perfect), and the support of early childhood professionals, children make progress toward the healthy resolution of these four developmental challenges:

- Trust versus mistrust during infancy

- Autonomy versus shame and doubt during toddlerhood

- Initiative versus guilt in the preschool years

- Industry versus inferiority during middle childhood

Notice that each challenge calls for the developing child to venture forth in life. But successful attainment of healthy levels of trust, autonomy, initiative, and industry only happens when the child experiences the safety net of positive relationships (Erikson 1963). Autonomy, initiative, and industry all require intentional action by the child and supportive reaction by the adult. (To this old duffer professor, the parallel is clear, with children needing to meet the first two safety-based democratic life skills in order to progress with the next three growth-based life skills.)

Through supportive relations (and consequent manageable stress), the child summons mastery motivation and engages in open-ended *mastery learning*—the expression of creativity. Creative learning experiences allow children to define for themselves whether the results of their efforts are gratifying. The following two scenarios illustrate creativity being suppressed and encouraged. Feel free to infer the effects of each teacher's response on the mastery motivation and the developing creativity of each child.

Scenario one: It had snowed. A teacher in one early childhood classroom read *Frosty the Snowman* to the children, and then they sang the song. The teacher showed the children a model of Frosty she had made and said they were all going to make their own Frosty. The children had patterns for the parts, but not all of them cut them out correctly. Many could not glue the parts just right on their blue papers. Some children asked, "Teacher, do it for me." Others just stopped working and tried to blend into the woodwork. A few older children, mainly girls, got fair approximations of Frosty. Two older boys were trying the best they could. One accidentally pasted the biggest circle in the middle. When the teacher came by, he said, "My

Frosty's been doing body building." The other boy got some markers, turned over his paper with the predrawn circles on it, and drew a ground line with a mound on it. He made the mound yellow. The teacher looked askance at the picture, and the boy said, "Teacher, we made a Frosty but the sun melted him, and my dog came and peed on it!" The two boys both showed remarkable (and charming) creativity in their pictures, but in the eyes of their teacher, they did them wrong.

Scenario two: It had snowed. The teacher in a second classroom talked about the snow with the children. She said that if the children came to the art table today, they could make their very own pictures of what they like to do outside in the snow. They could even write a story about it. She had paper with lines on the bottom for writing so the children could make their own *story pictures.* There were cotton balls and glue, chalk, markers, assorted paper scraps, and scissors for the children to use. Evette, fifty-eight months old, used the markers to draw three hills with trees between them. She drew a snowmobile on top of each hill, with two shapes representing family members on each snowmobile. She wrote on the lines, "M n m fm wt sn." (Me and my family went snowmobiling.) She was using invented, what some call developmental, spelling: a fundamental step in literacy development.

Sydney, forty-four months old, got white paper and began cutting circles. He got tape from the teacher and taped seventeen circles in a long row! With a marker, he drew a smiling face on the first one. When the teacher stopped by, Sydney stood up, showing his three-foot creation. He said, "This is a snow snake, Teacher, but don't worry. He's friendly. He won't bite."

All the children who came to the art table that day had unique creations. Most, like these two, had creative stories that went with them. The pictures were all different because the children were all different; they were all special because the children were all special. Please notice the power of spoken motivation by itself—setting a theme for the creative art—to unleash mastery motivation and mastery learning, even with preschoolers.

Most of the art that young children see in early childhood settings is art in picture books, telling stories. It is natural for children to follow this attractive modeling and create *story pictures,* pictures that tell stories. Open-ended art serves as the young child's blog, essay, poem, celebration, and lament—the child's gateway to self-expression on paper. Think of creative art as a pathway to healthy autonomy, initiative, and industry in early childhood classrooms. Think of it as vital lead-up activity for essays, compositions, and poems in the years to come.

When I once asked a little guy if he could tell me about his picture, he replied, "Dan, this is not a story to tell. It is a picture to look at." I then said what any hippie Head Start teacher would say: "Cool, man!" (These were the pre-"dude" days.) Still, with positive acknowledgment of detail and a pause, children will often tell you what their pictures are about. Think of it as language development that gives verbal expression to the *significant learning* children are doing through their creative activities and self-expressions on paper. A teacher commented to a toddler that her blue-marker circular scribble showed hard work. After a moment of hesitation, the child replied, "Yep, dis is my dad swimmin' with his swimsuit on." Glad the dude was wearing his budgie smuggler (Australian slang for swim togs).

Observation by graduate student, Randy: The children start arriving at kindergarten around 8:30 a.m., and I greet them as they come in. They seem very receptive to my greeting, and I watch them disperse to the different centers in the room. One boy is interested in striking up a conversation with me about a picture he has colored.

(*Lamar reaches out and hands me his picture.*)

RANDY: Wow! Looks like you used a lot of green.

LAMAR: Well, yeah, frogs are green.

RANDY: They are green, aren't they?

LAMAR: Yeah.

RANDY: You used green there for your frog and blue over there and brown over there. (*Lamar smiles.*)

LAMAR: Yep. I have a picture on the back too.

RANDY: What colors did you use?

LAMAR: I used different colors!

RANDY: I do see different colors! Yellow and pink and black. (*Lamar looks at me with a smile, gleaming with pride.*)

LAMAR: I will give you the picture that I colored.

RANDY: Thank you! I will put it on my fridge. (*Lamar peers up from his picture and smiles in amazement. He looks so pleased that I would put his picture up in my home.*)

Reflection: I was really nervous that I might give Lamar "good job" kind of praise instead of encouraging him to keep on with his good work. I like to praise people, and sometimes I have to be careful not to embarrass them and make them feel uncomfortable. When teachers begin to use encouragement, they sometimes find it difficult to know just what to say. Particularly when children's art is pre-representational, teachers can find themselves at a loss for words. I found myself feeling this way at first, and I tried to stay away from, "Oh, you are so good at coloring." I tried to look at Lamar's picture in a different way and to pick out things that were unique about it.

I saw that Lamar felt comfortable with the way the conversation went when he gave me his picture to take home. I knew then that he was proud of his work, and he seemed excited to show me other pictures he had colored. That day he sat by me during circle time.

The previous is from my May 2007 Guidance Matters column in *Young Children*. Thanks to NAEYC for permission to use this material.

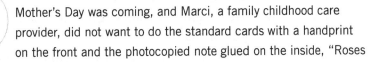 Mother's Day was coming, and Marci, a family childhood care provider, did not want to do the standard cards with a handprint on the front and the photocopied note glued on the inside, "Roses are red, violets are blue. It's Mother's Day, and I love you."

Instead, she cut paper of different light colors, folded the pieces into blank cards and encouraged the children to make their own cards for Mother's Day. Glynna, aged forty-two months, went to the art table and made a card. Very carefully on the front she drew big and little early pictorial figures holding hands, looking at each other, and smiling. (The figures were the familiar "heads" with appendages: legs, curls on Mom, smiling faces, and only the important arms.) Inside she made three lines of personal script (scribble writing) and signed her name with a *G*.

Marci complimented the details on Glynna's card and commented, "Not all adults can read children's writing. Would you like me to write down here what you wrote so your mother can read it?"

Glynna replied, "Yes. It says, 'It's Mother's Day, Mom, but I love you every day!'"

My challenge here to you is to cover up the pictures of realistic models on boxes of building materials, replace coloring books with blank paper, and put away the teacher-made models for children to copy. Instead, have children make their own creative pictures free of adult-imposed standards that they cannot yet meet. Provide spoken motivation and interesting materials. Let the children use their autonomy, initiative, and industry to create their own products. Over time you will see children's expressions on paper become more and more confident and creatively conventional. Smile then, for you have fostered mastery motivation, significant learning, and the successful expression of creativity.

Characteristic Five: Is Culturally Competent

As I see it, *cultural competence* means to be cognitively and socially responsive (intelligent and ethical) toward members of the early childhood community who may be different than the teacher physically, ethnically, culturally, religiously, and linguistically. Risking a stereotype to explain what I mean, a child from a family with an Asian heritage seems particularly driven to succeed in your classroom. The reaction by the early childhood professional is not "My goodness, these people all drive their kids so hard." It is "My goodness, this kid really seems driven. How can I help this child reach gratifying goals and still feel like a kid of worth just for who she is?" The answer most likely begins with building positive relationships with the child and also with family members.

Anti-bias education, the classic term used by Derman-Sparks and Edwards (2010), means that adults intentionally teach accepting responses toward others, whatever their unique human qualities. Teachers in particular need to model accepting responses toward children vulnerable for stigma (negative social separation from the group). Teachers reject the *power of silence*, the tendency to remain quiet in the face of oppressive interactions out of fear of "not saying the right thing" (York 2016).

Instead, with the child vulnerable for stigma, the adult practices *liberation teaching*, meaning never to give up on anyone in the teacher's charge. The teacher works actively to assist children at risk for stigma to overcome whatever vulnerabilities they may face. Issues of race, hygiene, disability, appearance, gender, and behavior—often precipitated by classroom conflicts—can all lead to one or more persons stigmatizing another. Stigmatizing means oppressing another in order to negatively separate that individual from the group—it is an assault on the other's ability to meet democratic life skill one (Gartrell 2012).

Two illustrations of anti-bias education through the use of liberation teaching follow. The illustrations address issues surrounding differences in race and gender.

In a campus child care center one day at lunch, four-year-old Martin (European American) comes to the table reluctantly when he sees that he will be sitting next to Brandon, who is American Indian. Martin says to Becca, an experienced student teacher, "I'm not sitting next to Brandon. He has dirty skin."

Becca gives Brandon a hug and whispers in his ear, "You don't have dirty skin, Brandon. People have different skin colors, and that's a good thing. I am going to talk with Martin."

Becca walks over to Martin, kneels next to him, and says, "Brandon's not dirty, Martin. He just has more color in his skin than you do. Lots of people have different skin colors, and that's a good thing. What's important in our class is that everyone is friendly to everyone." As she says this, she guides Martin to his chair and continues, "Brandon, could you pass the milk to Martin?" Brandon does, and Martin reluctantly thanks him. After rest time, Martin and Brandon play together, which puts a big smile on Becca's face.

Karla, the lead teacher, compliments Becca on her handling of the situation. Later that afternoon, when Martin's dad picks him up, Karla notices Becca talking with him quietly in the hallway. Afterward, Karla asks Becca what the conversation was about. Becca says, "I told him that Martin had said that another child who was American Indian had dirty skin. I thought Dad would want to know so he could reinforce what we tell the children in our class: people are born with different skin colors; that's natural, and what's important is that we are all friendly and get along."

The lead teacher reflects on whether a student teacher should be so bold in her comments to a parent. Karla concludes that by talking with the dad so forthrightly, Becca has done something that she herself would have found difficult to do—best the power of silence. When Martin arrives the next morning and plays again with Brandon, Karla recognizes the positive impact of Becca's liberation teaching.

In a classroom of four-year-olds, Stephon, Andrus, and Voshon play fireman, using the climber for the fire station and the dramatic play area for the house on fire. Stepping onto the climber, Charlene tries to join the play, but Stephon tells her, "You can't be a fireman 'cause you're a girl. Only boys can be firemen." Charlene scowls and nevertheless tries to join them on the climber, but the boys yell at her. Charlene sits on the floor and looks mad. Teacher Maya, who has seen the incident, sits down next to Charlene and puts her arm around her. "You look upset, Charlene."

With tears in her eyes, Charlene exclaims, "I want to play too! Girls can put out fires."

"Yes, they can, Charlene," Maya responds. "You are right. Both girls and boys can be firefighters. Let's talk to the boys."

They move to the climber, and Maya says, "Hey, guys, do you remember the book we read about firefighters? Men and women fight fires together. That's why we call them fire*fighters* instead of fire*men*." Stephon replies, "But this game is for boys, okay, Teacher?" Maya maintains an even, friendly tone in refuting this statement: "Our classroom agreement is that girls and boys play together. Charlene is unhappy that you don't want her to play with you. How can Charlene help you fight this fire?"

Stephon looks at the other two fire crew members and shrugs, "Charlene can steer on the back of the truck, 'cause you gotta steer there too. Look, a fire!" The four children race to the wooden bench that is the fire truck. Voshon hands Charlene a helmet. Charlene steers from the back, grinning.

While they are fighting the fire, Charlene notices two dolls, picks them up, and carries them to the fire truck. "I'm saving the babies," she calls out. "Charlene saved the babies!" the other firefighters shout. On the way back to the fire station, Charlene sits in the middle of the fire truck, proudly holding the babies she has saved. The four firefighters play together until cleanup time.

After cleanup, Maya has a quiet talk with Charlene and then with the three boys. The teacher reminds the children that women as well as men are firefighters. She compliments Charlene for thinking to save the babies and encourages the three boys to remember next time that girls and boys play together at school, including as firefighters.

Follow up: Maya talked with her coteacher, Margo, and the aide, Darius, about the incident. She told them how she had intervened when the boys wanted to exclude Charlene because she was a girl. The team agreed that the use of firm but friendly guidance in gender equality matters is important. Margo suggested that they discuss exclusion based on gender with the rest of the class. They decided to talk about it at group meeting the next day. Darius gave Maya contact information for a firefighter friend—a woman who had visited the school in the past.

The following week the firefighter visited the preschoolers. She arrived in street clothes and, with the class's participation, discussed, put on, and demonstrated her firefighting gear. The teacher took a picture of the class with the firefighter. The team put it up in the library corner, along with featured gender-balanced books about community helpers. That same day, Maya noticed Charlene and Della playing firefighters with two boys. The teacher was pleased that her guidance and liberation teaching had helped girls gain entry into boys' play and helped boys accept girls in their play.

Thanks to NAEYC for permission to reprint these anecdotes from the Guidance Matters columns in *Young Children*. Thanks also to Layna Cole, who cowrote the second column, "Guidance with Girls."

Cognitive Development in the Encouraging Learning Community

A possible criticism of this book is that too much attention is paid to emotional-social development and not enough to the cognitive domain. In this book we follow the maxim that a child must feel right to think and do right. A venerated viewpoint in early childhood education is that programs accommodate the *whole child*, including being respectful of emotional and social factors in children's lives (Copple and Bredekamp 2009). All children, and especially young children, learn holistically. They learn best when developmental domains can be engaged together, beginning with the child's emotional and social realities.

We return here to John Dewey's essential point: education curricula, whether formally spelled out or not, are necessarily logical (Dewey 1966). Broad goals and outcomes are broken down into objectives and lessons, and organized around general principles such as moving from simple to the complex. But children are psychological beings, not automatons. They learn psychologically, not logically, through immediate, hopefully gratifying, minute-by-minute experiences. They integrate their cognitive learning into the developmental dynamic that is at the core of their beings, constantly changing their brain physiology in the process.

The professional teacher works hard every day to make the logical trappings of the curriculum—the schedule, materials, planned activities, physical environment, and even assessment processes—relevant for the children in the group. Dewey indicated that in this way, the curriculum emerges in conjunction with the growing experiences and interests of the children. For me, this practice is the essence of what developmentally appropriate education is about. Significant cognitive learning happens, but it happens organically, as a key but integrated process within the dynamic development of the child.

Edna, aged forty-seven months, lags behind her mates who are taking a sidewalk field trip along a busy street to a park. Walking with the group, I stay back with her. As they approach a corner, student teacher Byron comes back for Edna. The group waits. Byron finds Edna bent over, walking in circles, watching an ant! He acknowledges her activity to her, then helps her catch up to the group.

When they reach the park, Byron has a safety guidance talk with Edna. Recognizing that this is a level one mistaken behavior, Byron reminds Edna of the guideline to stay with the group. But he also says, "You were really observing that ant, weren't you?" Edna says, "Yep, I like ants. They are busy, busy, busy." Byron later talks with the lead teacher about the incident. She grins broadly, shakes her head, and says, "That's Edna, always busy doing her own thing, just like the ants!"

The next day, Byron brings in an ant farm and library books on insects for Edna and the other children to study. With some of the others in the group, Byron and Edna collect bugs on the playground, look them up in the books, and make story pictures about them in their science journals. (Byron explains why they can't add the bugs to the ant farm—it is a peaceable classroom.) Neither adult can remember seeing Edna so happy in program activities, joined by her equally engaged friends.

For guidance professionals like Byron and his lead teacher, Edna's interest in ants was commendable, just not shown at the right time. (A technician response to Edna would have been to ignore Edna's pursuit and just scold her about leaving the line.) To my mind, emergent curriculum insect activities with the group the next day means that these pros made this lime into not just limeade, but key lime pie—not just for Edna, but for the other children in the group.

Willingness to Engage

The hallmark of developmentally appropriate education is children's ability and willingness to engage with the logical structures of the curriculum and to experience meaningful, even if not always successful, learning outcomes. Settings where this learning happens are encouraging learning communities. We can say that in these settings, all children

- are making progress with democratic life skills one and two: they have gained enough of a sense of self and an ability to manage emotions to be able to interact mostly productively with others.

- are intrigued enough by materials and activities to fully engage (activate *mastery motivation*) in the learning process.

- through full engagement are beginning to work on DLS 3, 4, and 5: solving problems creatively, individually, and with others; accepting unique human qualities in others; beginning to act in intelligent and ethical ways.

In an encouraging learning community, children feel intrigued enough to engage in learning activities and gratified enough by the experience that the positive learning stays with them into the future. The following two illustrations involving music experiences show teachers working hard to build an encouraging learning community for the children in their care.

 Music illustration one: A fifty-month-old sister and a thirty-nine-month-old brother moved with their family from a largely Ojibwe community to a relatively diverse university town in northern Minnesota. In the preschool they began attending, the group was using early childhood band instruments. Handed rhythm sticks, Jodi and Cheyenne each put one stick down. Instead of hitting the sticks together, they each hit their single stick on the floor in time with the music. Cheyenne appeared to cup an ear with his free hand.

Assistant teacher Betty, from the same Ojibwe community, recognized that the sister and brother were using the sticks as if to beat on a ceremonial drum. She contained a chuckle. Later Betty and teacher Kristin discussed the children's unique manner of using the rhythm sticks. Betty spoke with the children's parents.

A few days later, Kristin explained to the group that they were going to have some special visitors—Jodi and Cheyenne's father and older sister—who were going to share the kind of music that was special to the two children and their family. Dad brought in a drum, played it, and sang in Ojibwe. Louella, the older sister, wore her special jingle dress—which she changed into after she met the class—and danced. Everyone was given rhythm sticks, and led by Jodi and Cheyenne, they beat them on the floor in time to the music. Many children and the adults danced with Louella.

Music illustration two: When she handed out band instruments for group music time, preschool teacher Kristin noticed that the children often argued over who got what. She also noticed that some children were particularly interested in using the instruments and didn't want to hand them back in at the end of the sessions. Because the program was located in a church basement with smaller rooms next to their large space, Kristin and Betty got permission to set up an adjacent small room as a music room, open during choice times when an adult was present.

In the room, the teachers placed band instruments, a keyboard with headphones (the volume preset to a safe level), a five-gallon plastic bucket upside down, and drumsticks. They wanted the children interested in making music to have significant learning experiences. This meant not five-minute timers by the different instrument groups for turns, but a sign-up sheet completed before choice time. Individuals who signed up for an instrument could use it for up to the entire choice time that day. When they were done, they found the next person on the list.

Jodi, Cheyenne, and a variety of other children often chose to use the drum (accompanied by recordings of Ojibwe ceremonial songs). One child in particular, Zelda, fifty-four months old, liked to play the keyboard and did so every time she could sign up for it. Betty and Kristin were impressed to discover that before long, Zelda was actually playing chords and the beginnings of a simple song or two. They let Zelda's mom know, who promised to find a preschool music class for her outside of school.

The two illustrations show teachers mediating between the logical curriculum and the psychological child, using emergent curriculum to build an encouraging learning community. Developmentally appropriate education allows the child to enact *mastery motivation*—the intrinsic motivation characteristic of DLS 3, 4, and 5 (Reineke, Sonsteng, and Gartrell 2008). The sustained interest and engagement with the activity results in *mastery learning*—optimum, gratifying brain development through the learning experience.

Mastery learning happens only with in-depth experiences that are repeated until the child feels a sense of mastery for what he or she can do with a material. When mastery learning is occurring, the child's attention span for an activity often grows longer than the adult's! (Think of how many times you have read the same book to the same child in the same sitting. Who got tired of the book first?) Smile when you have this experience; on this day, for this child, you have created an encouraging learning community.

Significant Learning

We can use Carl Rogers's term *significant learning* to link gratifying learning experiences in the present with the future life of the child (Rogers 1961). Significant learning stays with the child beyond the context of the original learning. Examples of this in the above illustrations are a sustaining music experience that relates to one's culture and family values and a positive mastery experience with a material (the keyboard) that creates a possible new pathway for future development.

An encouraging community that empowers mastery motivation, leading to mastery learning, is the key to long-term significant learning (Reineke, Sonsteng, and Gartrell 2008). Think of adults who loved to play with Legos as kids and now are builders, who loved bugs and now are entomologists, who loved reading and writing and now are serial readers and writers, and who loved music and now are musicians. In the encouraging community, the significant learning that a child does on any day may stay with that child and have an impact on the arc of her or his entire life. Early childhood professionals teach not just for a given day but for a lifetime.

Encouraging Learning Communities: Teaching and Learning for Life in a Modern Democracy

Empowered mastery motivation, mastery learning, and significant learning happen best in encouraging learning communities. The term *community* is key here. Young children need to identify with the groups with whom they share their young lives. An early childhood education definition for a community is a group that shares relationships, values, practices, experiences, and customs in a culture of togetherness. While maybe not *always* as enthusiastically as a cheerleader, the guidance professional works unrelentingly to build group spirit inclusive of all. The teacher leaves this indelible message with each member of the community: you are special just because you are in our group.

Within the education field, programs that take on the mission to be encouraging learning communities tend to be participants in *progressive education.* For many educators, past and present, progressive education is about preparing children to be healthy individuals and informed, productive citizens in a democratic society. To the extent that they can in this age of "no child left untested," progressive educators focus on helping children gain democratic life skills more than high scores on standardized tests measuring academic performance.

Standardized tests are the epitome of technician-driven schooling—socializing students for life in what kind of society? In contrast, minimally invasive *authentic assessment* systems record and analyze actual samples of children's work and are in harmony with what progressive education is about. Through assessment methods, developmentally appropriate practice, and guidance leadership, early childhood professionals provide the members of the encouraging learning community with a foundation for healthy, informed, and productive living in the many communities that form this complex democratic society.

We sometimes think of the early learning community as comprising the children and one or two early childhood professionals. The early learning community includes much more: every staff member, family member, volunteer, consulting professional, and visitor that has contact with the group. The adult in charge—whether lead teacher, classroom manager, or family child care provider-in-chief—works to include all in the community. In fact, many of the guidance practices in the following chapters can be used with adult members of the community as well as children.

Discussion Questions

An element of being an early childhood professional is respecting the children, parents, and educators with whom you are working by keeping identities private. In completing follow-up activities, please respect the privacy of all concerned.

1. Think of a young child who began in a program working on DLS 1 or 2. If that child progressed to working on DLS 3, 4, or 5, how did an adult's relationship with that child make a difference?

2. If that child progressed to working on DLS 3, 4, or 5, what part do you think the day-to-day educational program played in helping the child to progress?

3. If that same child failed to make progress in gaining DLS 1 or 2, what do you think were some challenges the child and/or teacher could not overcome?

4. Think about a creative activity with which one or more children in a group were totally engaged. What do you remember about the effort the children exerted? About the resulting product or accomplishment? For one or two children, what can you surmise about the mastery learning that might have resulted? About the significant learning that might have resulted?

Key Concepts

Definitions of the Key Concepts can be found in the glossary on pages 177–84.

Anti-bias education	Liberation teaching
Authentic assessment	Mastery learning
Cultural competence	Power of silence
Encouraging learning community	Significant learning
Family groups	Story pictures

CHAPTER 4

Working with Families on Behalf of the Child

HISTORICALLY, A WIDESPREAD PRACTICE in American schooling was to consider the child entering the classroom as separate from the child at home (Souto-Manning and Swick 2006). School personnel made this judgment from the prevalent belief that the institution of the school was a "social improvement" over life for the child in the family (Manger 1980). This unfortunate attitude is a remnant of the historical melting-pot function of American schools (Crawford and Zygourias-Coe 2006).

Between the end of the Civil War and the beginning of World War II, immigrants, often from southern and eastern Europe, more than doubled the U.S. population. Many of the newcomers spoke little English and knew little of American life (Manger 1980). During this time, for political more than educational reasons, schools were charged with "Americanizing the aliens" (Locke 1919). Teachers of the younger grades were urged by the Department of the Interior to take on the role of acculturating immigrant mothers through home visits, meetings, and conferences (female immigrants were seen as being socialized as citizens through the workplace). The thinking was that individuals of various backgrounds would thus be assimilated into a common culture and form the great melting pot of American society.

However, as a result of the social norm of the melting pot, many immigrant parents, as well as parents from American minority groups, felt that they were "surrendering" their children to the schools and giving up important rights and responsibilities as parents (Quiocho and Daoud 2006).

Janet Gonzalez-Mena, along with authors cited above, points out that this national error in judgment (my words) undermines young children's natural

This chapter is a reworking of chapter 6 in *Education for a Civil Society: How Guidance Teaches Young Children Democratic Life Skills* using my original notes. Thanks to NAEYC for permission to adapt that material for this chapter.

identification with their families, as well as their personal identities as family members (2008). It tends to place school influence and family influence at odds in children's minds, putting children in the difficult position of having to choose between two sometimes competing cultures. Many families accepted the sacrifices involved in giving their children over to the schools to be "Americanized." But other families found these sacrifices difficult to endure.

"Say, Dan," Big Ben said, "you know what comes after Indian summer, don't you?" When I taught Head Start for the Red Lake Ojibwe in northern Minnesota, a guy we'll call Ben was a janitor. The children were drawn to Big Ben, and he teased them gently in ways that made them smile. I knew I was in for it with his question, and, shaking my head, I told him I didn't know. "White man winter!" Ben boomed with a wide grin.

Ben is gone now, but I got to know him well enough at Head Start to admire his quick mind and the fact that this sixth-grade-educated janitor spoke four languages. At home in his early childhood, Ben spoke Ojibwe, the language of his family. At age six, he was taken to the reservation boarding school, about ten miles from his home. At the school, where he was required to live most of the year, Ben was physcially punished if he spoke his native language. Ben learned English quickly enough but still spoke Ojibwe to his friends when he thought he wouldn't get caught.

At age twelve, Ben was allowed to leave the boarding school and return home. He found work with a German American farmer near the west end of the reservation and soon learned German. Stationed in France during World War II, Ben picked up conversational French. I sometimes heard him sharing his linguistic gifts with those around him.

When I mentioned the janitor in one of my university classes, a student commented that Ben could have been a one-man language department at a high school or college. I agreed that with support he could have been, but instead Ben was the victim of an almost four-hundred-year cultural war waged against native families. Two students in the class then spoke up. One mentioned that her grandmother had not been allowed to start school in northeastern Minnesota until she spoke English instead of Lithuanian. Another mentioned that his grandfather had been paddled by a teacher when he spoke Finnish at school.

For children whose family backgrounds and values are similar to the teacher's, the cultural school-home conflict is less extreme. For children whose home culture is noticeably different from the school's, this cultural dilemma was—and for many families, often still is—significant indeed (Quiocho and Daoud 2006).

Early Childhood Education: A Gentle Force for Inclusion

Early childhood educators have long understood the importance of school and home working together. Froebel emphasized the need for home visits and mothers' meetings. In the Casa dei Bambini, Montessori held that regular mother-directress meetings were essential to children's progress. She encouraged directresses to invite mothers into the schools to observe.

Moving beyond the expectation that mothers would be the ones involved in their children's education, James Hymes (1974) is among those who first began to frame effective home-school relations (as the title of his book calls it) in more inclusive terms. Coming from a tradition of early childhood education as a service to families, Hymes was, with Edward Zigler and others, a key person in the founding of Head Start. My particular approach to building *reciprocal relationships* is clearly influenced by my involvement with Head Start, but hopefully this chapter successfully adapts that approach to early care and childhood education as a whole.

Nowadays, parents mostly recognize the importance of children's formative years and of positive adult-child relationships during those years. Early childhood professionals build partnerships with families and helping relationships with children to keep the children's two worlds connected and secure. This is why NAEYC's position statement on developmentally appropriate practice so thoroughly documents the importance of family-teacher partnerships, particularly when families and early childhood professionals come from different cultural backgrounds (NAEYC 2009). The encouraging early childhood community expands on the child's home life without trying to replace it (Gonzalez-Mena 2006).

In 2009 Halgunseth and colleagues published the NAEYC document *Family Engagement, Diverse Families, and Early Childhood Education Programs: An Integrated Review of the Literature.* The report details how schools historically viewed parent involvement from a deficit model: the purpose of parent involvement with the school was to correct implicit weaknesses in the family that might detract from the child's education. The contemporary model, delineated in the report, is strengths based: the family and teacher, through reciprocal relationships, combine their separate knowledge and skills to forge together a positive education for the child. Beyond the early childhood years, these partnerships are essential for the healthy development and successful education of older learners as well. At any level, the relationship needs to be reciprocal. *Such partnerships are the role of the teacher to initiate and sustain.*

Accepting Diversity

In chapter 3, we discussed how teachers should respond to ethnic, racial, and gender diversity, showing how these human differences can put children in the learning setting at risk for stigma. Here we look at two other dimensions of human difference ever more common in today's complex society: linguistic and religious. These dimensions can affect interactions at both teacher-child and teacher-family levels. Early childhood professionals who accept diversity are working at the high-level democratic life skill four—accepting differing human qualities in others. These teachers model the skill even as they teach it to others.

Linguistic Diversity: A Second Language Is a Gift

Cultural diversity in its many forms is becoming ever more visible in American communities. One of these forms is linguistic diversity. According to a 2010 US Census Bureau report, a growing number of families in the United States speak a language other than English in the home—19.7 percent in 2007 (Shin and Kominski 2010). With families whose home language is not English, teachers work to build strong relationships and to make them feel welcome in the setting. Nemeth (2012) suggests the following practices for effectively including children whose home languages are not English:

- If possible, have parents spend some time in the setting with the child.

- On signs and displays, use pictures and languages that reflect children's home cultures and languages.

- Learn a few words in the children's home languages. Ask families for assistance with these words and look for translations of words online.

- Reflect each child's language and culture throughout the setting—in children's books, on labels, on dolls, and in toys. Add foods and cooking tools that are familiar to the children to the kitchen area.

Nemeth also offers several suggestions for conducting conferences with parents who do not speak English or whose English is uncertain, particularly when challenging topics arise. These suggestions supplement recommendations for parent-teacher conferences later in the chapter.

- Seek to establish a positive relationship with families before a challenging situation arises. Share photos and videos of children's activities with parents.

- Have an interpreter attend a conference. If it is not possible to include a certified interpreter, ask a trusted member of the staff or family to help. Seek out individuals from community organizations who are knowledgeable about a family's culture and language—and, to the extent possible, early childhood education.

- Promote mutual understanding using aids such as a message board with photos and words in both English and the family's home language. Teachers and parents can point to what they wish to communicate.

- Keep information brief and clear to avoid overwhelming parents and to increase the chances that they will understand the most critical points you want to convey.

- Resolve differences together. To understand a family's concerns and priorities, it is vital that teachers get to know family members and what is important to them.

Through each of the communication practices, the teacher remains "unrelentingly positive" (Marian Marion's term) in efforts to form reciprocal relationships with all families and to encourage their engagement in furthering their child's learning in the home as well as school.

Teachers who view *dual-language learning* as a lasting neuropsychological gift for children embrace this cultural strength in participating families (Genishi and Dyson 2009).

Language immersion elementary schools and early childhood education programs—along with language immersion camps such as the internationally known Concordia Language Villages in Minnesota—are beginning to bring this aspect of American education into a new century. An August 7, 2011, *Newsweek* article by Casey Schwartz, "Why It's Smart to be Bilingual," reports that 440 schools (up from virtually none in 1970) offered language immersion programs. The American Council on the Teaching of Foreign Languages (2011) contends that beginning dual-language learning during early childhood even results in benefits for brain development, functioning, and alertness in old age. In my view, this research points the way forward for a vital American trend.

Religious Diversity: A Matter of Beliefs

Linguistic diversity can be challenging for teachers—perhaps in one way if one family has a home language other than English, perhaps in another way if several different languages are spoken (such as the eight languages spoken in a St. Paul kindergarten I recently visited). A sometimes-vexing issue for teachers is when linguistic differences are coupled with differences in religious beliefs between teachers and one or more participating families. Whatever the specifics, cultural responsiveness in matters of religion always comes down to open acceptance on the part of the teacher.

The profile that follows is compiled from papers written by two Minnesota teachers who were graduate students in my classes some years ago. Their experiences were remarkably similar, so with their permission, I've blended them in the following study. Mary Beth (not her real name) recalls her experience with a family that other teachers had found difficult to work with.

 In my first year, a teacher told me to watch out for a certain family whose younger child was to be in my kindergarten class. The family members were Jehovah's Witnesses, and as part of their faith, they had taught their children not to salute the flag nor celebrate birthdays and holidays.

This teacher told me that in the previous year the parents had become irate when they were not told of a Halloween party in their older child's classroom, even though their child had not participated. From then on, the teacher tried to let the family know of upcoming events, but she felt they remained distant and uncooperative.

There were instances when the older child, now a third grader, had been made fun of by classmates. Arlys, the mother, had reported these incidents, but the teacher apparently told the family that there was not much she could do.

I took this teacher's comments as a personal challenge, and I decided to work hard to reach out to this family. It was my practice to send home notes of introduction to each family before school began and then continue with happygrams (notes to families complimenting children's efforts) on a rotating basis for each member of my class. I made sure the child, Wilma, went home with at least one happygram every week. This was not a hard task, as I enjoyed the child's pluckiness. I read her each note before giving it to her to bring home. I called the home a few times as well, but I always got an answering machine. I left messages that I hoped the parents would find friendly.

Other teachers told me not to expect this family to attend the fall parent conference, but Arlys did come. I was very pleased to see this mother, and she seemed rather surprised at my reaction. I decided to let Arlys bring up issues related to their religion. My job was to let her know that I valued working with families and that her daughter was doing well in my class. Well, she did bring it up. I told her I was interested to hear about her faith (because I was).

Arlys told me about the flag salute, and I said not to worry—we wouldn't be doing the flag salute until close to the end of the year because I didn't think the children could understand it. She smiled at this. About birthdays, I told her what I told all the parents: I preferred that the children had parties at home, but we let the children wear a birthday crown for the day if that was okay with the parents. Arlys said no crown for Wilma, but otherwise she liked what I did.

I asked Arlys what she would like me to do about holiday activities, and we had quite a conversation about that. I was very surprised when she said Wilma could stay in the classroom if I could figure out a way to have her fit in without participating. That year I kind of downplayed the holidays, explaining to parents who asked that not all of the children in the class celebrated all holidays. I did more with the ideas behind the holidays. For instance, rather than holding Thanksgiving pageants and having the children make crafts, I had the class consider why we should be thankful. This is a practice I still use today.

What I am still the proudest about with this family has to do with the flag salute. Before we started saluting the flag in April, I asked three parents to come in to discuss with the class what saluting the flag meant to them. One was Arlys, and she did a fine job of explaining why Wilma would stand up out of respect for the class but wouldn't be doing the rest. (All three parents knew that they were part of a panel and that the three might be expressing different opinions about the salute.) I do not remember any of the children making fun of Wilma that whole year—they liked her, just as I did.

As I said, the matter comes down to openness toward the belief systems of others— whatever those sources of faith happen to be. The young child in the learning setting is always an extension of, and informally a representative of, the family. Appreciation of the family's linguistic and religious heritage is a foremost step in accepting the child.

Building Trust through Communication

The early childhood professional's goal with family members is mutual trust. As teachers learn more about the children's families and as family members learn more about the teacher and the program, they begin to work together on behalf of the children. Establishing this level of cooperation early is essential. A teacher does not want the first significant contact with a parent to be over scratches or bite marks caused or received by the parent's child. With a trust level built, when children encounter problems, the focus is more likely on resolving the matter than on recriminations about who is to blame.

Here are five suggestions for practices that enable cooperative communication and partnerships with children's family members.

1. Digital Communication Comes Naturally to *Most*

Just as readers likely did, most young families today grew up with Facebook, Twitter, YouTube, Snapchat, e-mail, interactive websites, texting, and the other latest means of electronic connection. The digital divide remains real, however, for both families in financial distress and families who abstain from digital communication on principle. Some families just plain will not be digitally connected. The teacher needs to make sure those who do not use technology will not be disadvantaged in teacher-parent communication.

Through greeting meetings at the beginning of the school year, informal survey letters, and early conferences, teachers can discover which parents are and are not users of (which) digital technology. One way is to ask parents if they would prefer e-mails or physical notes sent home, and if they would prefer hard-copy newsletters or a regularly updated website. If necessary, teachers can print out and send home web pages, including the photos of kids in action that electronic media have made so easy to work with. Teachers might find that some families would appreciate classes or assistance with technology use. Providing such assistance is another way to build relationships with families.

2. Written Notes, Even in the Digital Age

Many adults associate notes sent home with critical messages from the teacher. In encouraging learning communities, however, the reasons for notes are to announce events and to build relationships with families. Relationship notes should be either happygrams (notes complimentary of a child's efforts) or progress statements as follow-up to a conference. Because children wonder about the content of personal notes from the teacher, teachers might read them to the child before sending them home. If the tone of the note is encouraging, children generally take pride in seeing that it is delivered. Even though there is a significant place for electronic communication between school and home, your grandmother was right: a friendly note does what digital communication cannot.

3. Phone Calls Allow for Connection

Telephone calls to families are more direct than e-mails and notes. Just about everybody has a cell phone. Many teachers call or text parents regularly. Especially with parents who are nonreaders, phone calls allow for important connections. However, there is a note of privilege associated with being given a parent's phone number, and gaining this access should be handled respectfully. Perhaps during first conferences, gently inquire about each family's preferences regarding phone contacts.

Phone calls allow for actual conversation but not for physical proximity and face-to-face contact. So, under normal circumstances, I don't recommend that a teacher conduct a serious conference on the phone; instead, use the call to set up a time to meet with the caregiving family member.

Phones are useful for establishing and maintaining relationships with families, for delivering happygram messages via texts, for following up on parent-teacher conferences, and for other purposes that you work out with the family. If the teacher wants to communicate more directly than with a note (or even a phone text), a friendly phone call still means a lot to a parent.

Some teachers use a phone answering machine as an electronic hub for their programs. On a schedule known to families, they record the latest assignments, upcoming events, and do-together ideas for families, which parents can access at their leisure. Other teachers post phone call-in times when they are available to speak to families about their needs and concerns.

4. Home Visits Build Relationships

Early childhood programs of all kinds benefit from home visits, especially during start-up with new families and at the beginning of the program year. Home visits help teachers learn about family dynamics and children's response styles in ways that aren't possible in the confines of the child care setting. Home visits are also opportunities for teachers to learn about the cultural contexts of families so they can make decisions about what is culturally relevant for the children in their class.

Some programs, including Head Start, have staff members who are full-time home visitors. Head Start home visitors work with both family members and child, acting informally as social workers as well as early childhood teachers. On a visit, these early childhood education professionals typically meet with parents first, bringing activities for the child (and siblings) to do. They also guide parents and children in activities together, sometimes modeling teaching the child in the home.

Home visitors actively encourage family members to participate in services the program—and the community—have to offer. They work cooperatively with families in this effort, endeavoring first to build trusting reciprocal relations. Programs need to establish and communicate clear policies that spell out what is and is not part of home visit activities. Any early childhood setting can benefit greatly if it can build home visits into its program.

The following reprint of part of a Guidance Matters column shows how a Head Start home visitor, over time, was able to build a reciprocal relationship with a parent and encourage a high level of engagement in this Head Start program. For the column, I interviewed parent Cathryn and home visitor Kay in Cathryn's home.

Cathryn, a twenty-seven-year-old mother of three, enrolled in Mahube Head Start in northwestern Minnesota as a single mom six years ago. Living with her parents at the time, Cathryn signed up for Mahube's Early Head Start/Pregnant Moms program. Ever since her first child, Curtis, was born, Cathryn has worked with Kay, who makes regular home visits and facilitates weekly parent-child group sessions with Cathryn and other families in the community. Cathryn has since married, and her husband, Don, is a dental lab technician. Now age five, Curtis has graduated from Early Head Start to a preschool center-based Head Start classroom that meets four days a week. Sisters Kyrie (nearly three) and Elizabeth (six months) are still with their mom in Early Head Start, led by Kay.

Cathryn says that when she began in the program she was shy and in her shell. She knew little about raising a child, not even what questions to ask Kay and the other Early Head Start staff members. From the time he could crawl, Curtis has been an on-the-go child, very active every moment he is awake. Gradually, Cathryn became more comfortable discussing her son with Kay. His activity level really stood out for Cathryn when younger sister Kyrie showed behaviors that were night-and-day different from Curtis.

Because of her relationship with Kay, Cathryn decided to follow Kay's suggestion and have Curtis assessed for ADHD and related emotional issues. Curtis is now in his second year attending a weekly therapeutic play group as well as the regular Head Start classroom on the four other days. Cathryn stays in close contact with Curtis's teachers, as she says, "because I am the authority when it comes to my son, and I know him best. We talk together about planning ways to deal with any problems he has."

Kay and Cathryn agree that she was far from this point in her development as a parent when Curtis was younger. Cathryn indicates her pride in being able to form partnerships with teachers regarding Curtis and his needs. Cathryn and Don have decided that Curtis will attend a nearby community school next year rather than the large town school where they live. Head Start staff is providing support with the transition so the parents can start a new close relationship with the public school teaching staff and continue assisting Curtis through a coordinated approach to positive guidance.

Cathryn is an informal leader during Kay's weekly parent-child sessions. (She shares that she has given suggestions to younger parents regarding meal and bedtime routines.) This year she was elected to the Head Start Advisory Council and travels forty miles one way to attend meetings. "I know how much children gain from Head Start," Cathryn says, "but Head Start also helps parents like me grow in their confidence as parents and people." Kay told me earlier that Cathryn is a star Head Start parent, is grounded, and has a definite purpose in life. I see all of this during the interview.

5. Family-Teacher Conferences Foster Engagement

Except for home visits, conferences provide the most direct link between teacher and parent. Much has been written in recent years about parent-teacher conferences (Gestwicki 2015; Gonzalez-Mena 2008). Gonzalez-Mena emphasizes that early childhood professionals need to see themselves as learners as well as teachers, especially when cultural differences, including a home language other than English, are involved. Gestwicki explains that successful conferences consist of three phases: *preparing*, *conducting*, and *evaluating*.

Preparing

When preparing, the teacher needs to make sure parents know the reasons for the conference. A program guidebook can include a statement about conferences that is repeated in follow-up communication. As appropriate, this information should be in the home languages of the program's children and families. Time options are helpful for parents, including both nighttime and daytime slots if possible. An informal, private setting, in which parents and teacher can sit side by side at a table, is preferable to conversing across a desk. Teachers should plan adequate time for the discussion so parents do not feel hurried.

 In a primary school, a mother named Jocelyn shared with the teacher that her husband, Voshon, literally had a gag reflex when he entered the doors of the school—which he had attended—due to his own distressing experiences as a student. The teacher suggested that they have the initial conference in a neighborhood fast-food restaurant. Jocelyn got Voshon to attend, and the teacher emphasized her positive perceptions of how their son, Torri, was doing. Dad later decided he could make the next conference in the classroom—the teacher had communicated clearly and consistently to him that their son was an accepted and respected member of the class.

Providing a comfortable setting for parent conferences is crucial. At one parent's suggestion, a teacher held conferences in a small parents' corner already established in the room. The corner included bulletin board dividers, two easy chairs, and a coatrack. The parents loved the change.

The teacher should have a folder or portfolio for each child with samples of the child's work over time, including photographs of the child's activities and projects. Dated observational notes are helpful. Some teachers may include video clips of the child at work, shared via a laptop or computer screen (better than tiny-screened personal devices). This strategy is particularly useful when holding conferences with families of children who are dual-language learners. A form to record notes from the conference rounds out this stage (Gestwicki 2015).

Conducting

For the conduct of the conference, the teacher sets the tone with positive statements about the child, such as, "I really enjoy having Natisha in class. She works hard and has such a sense of humor." The teacher asks the parents to share what they would like to see the conference accomplish. The teacher goes over the materials she has prepared and invites the parents to discuss them. When the teacher talks about the child, she or he uses the technique known as the *compliment sandwich*—giving at least two positive statements about the child's effort and progress that frame one suggestion for further growth (see page 130 for more on compliment sandwiches).

The teacher also encourages family members to share information about their child's home life. She or he acknowledges the parents' comments and uses *reflective listening*, which means repeating back the thoughts and feelings the other person is expressing (Pappano 2007). Reflective listening helps ensure that the parents' messages have been received as intended. As the conference wraps up, the teacher summarizes decisions made and any follow-up plans, checking to make sure family members agree. The teacher ends the conference on a positive note (Gestwicki 2015).

An important trend in conferencing for children at all age levels is to include the learner along with the parents. Teachers' first reactions to this idea can be guarded; they (and the parents) may have to approach both the material and the communication process differently with the learner present. After teachers get used to this format, they commonly say that under most circumstances they wouldn't have conferences any other way. Often a young child will sit in on part of the conference, then be free to play in the room if the discussion gets too involved.

Evaluating

Following the conference, the teacher evaluates the session by reviewing notes and completing a brief summary. She or he files the original form and sends a copy to the parents—in their home language, if possible. The teacher reflects in personal terms about the success of the conference, carries through on agreed-on follow-up actions, and initiates plans for conferences to come.

It can be tempting to regard the meeting and its evaluation as the conclusion of the effort to build productive relations with families, but collaborative teacher-parent relations are an ongoing effort. When early childhood professionals carry through with follow-ups and further conferences, they show they understand the importance of family in the life of the child and the child in the life of the family.

Gestwicki concludes her discussion of conferences with this point:

> It should be remembered that nonattendance at a conference does not necessarily indicate disinterest in the child or the school. Instead, it may be a reflection of different cultural or socioeconomic values, of extreme pressures or stress [on the] family or work demands. A teacher's response to nonattendance is to review the possible explanations, see if different scheduling or educational action will help, persist in invitations and efforts, and understand that other methods of reaching a parent will have to be used in the meantime. (2015, 341)

Levels of Family Engagement

In developing their parent engagement model, Halgunseth and her colleagues (2009) built on Epstein's (2001) work on assessing parent engagement in school programs. I've also used Epstein's material, modifying her criteria as four *levels of family engagement*. Parents become able to progress through the levels when they feel trust and reliability in their relationships with early childhood professionals. Such relationships help teachers understand and respond to children's behavior with appropriate guidance strategies for building the democratic life skills. Through partnerships, the teacher supports family members in reinforcing the life skills in the home as well.

The four levels are as follows:

Level One: Acceptance of program information

Level Two: Active educational engagement with one's child

Level Three: Active program participation

Level Four: Personal/professional development

Families differ in the level of participation they are ready to engage in (Halgunseth et al. 2009). In some early childhood programs, teachers and family members work together most often at engagement levels one and two; in other programs, they may work together at levels one through three or four. To illustrate the levels, I refer to Mary Beth's experience with Arlys and Wilma, on pages 72–73 (Study One); and to Kay and Cathryn's long-time collaboration on pages 76–77 (Study Two).

Level One: Accepting Program Information

Showing unconditional acceptance, the teacher warmly introduces family members and children to the program. Most families, if they feel accepted, are willing to participate at level one, at least accepting information about the program and what their child is doing and learning. Level one extends to attending meetings, conferences, and class events as the parent can find the time. The teacher makes the most of this willingness, recognizing the two sources of information that families have: the *teacher* and the *child*.

On the teacher's part, he or she uses the methods of communication mentioned as well as parent meetings. The teacher works for three outcomes at this first level of involvement:

1. The family member understands that the teacher accepts and appreciates the child.

2. The family member feels comforted by communicating with the teacher about family background, including information about the child.

3. The family member becomes willing to increase involvement.

In relation to the child, the attitude of the child toward school makes all the difference in the willingness of the family to become engaged with the program. If the child wants to come to school "even when sick," the teacher can conclude that the foundation is being set for further family engagement. If the child "does not want to come to school when well," participation limited to the passive receipt of information—or even the rejection of information—is all the teacher can expect. A welcoming approach by early childhood professionals toward both child and family allows the family to progress in the levels of engagement.

In Study One, Mary Beth did not let herself be influenced by the other teachers' attitudes toward the family. She enjoyed having Wilma in class and conveyed this acceptance quietly and consistently to her. She sent home happygrams and left positive phone messages about Wilma for the family. On Wilma's part, she quickly came to enjoy kindergarten and her teacher—she wouldn't miss a day. When the mother attended a first conference, Mary Beth showed friendliness to Arlys and a genuine interest in Wilma and the family, including the family's religious values. That Arlys responded to the teacher's friendly inclusiveness by attending the conference showed that she had moved past feelings of alienation from the school to engagement at level one.

Level Two: Active Educational Engagement with One's Child

Engagement at level two means that parents move from accepting information about their child to positively acting on the information received. Typically, families at level two follow up on activities and projects begun or assigned. Perhaps even more important, families use more fully the resources in the home and community as teaching and learning opportunities for their child. Teachers help families muster available resources and reach out for additional resources to further support their children's learning (NAEYC 2009).

In helping families move from level one to level two, the teacher's goal is to motivate families to use parenting practices that further children's education and learning in and around the home. Encouraging an extension of classroom practices, such as reading to the child each day, is an important component of this communication. The teacher works with the family to help family members see their everyday activities as essentially educational for children. For example, an adult might take the child on the bus or subway that the adult rides to work or to shop, or the adult and child might drive to interesting locations, go on walks, or do household chores. The teacher helps parents understand the importance of adults talking with children during these activities.

At level two, mutual trust is growing, and parents begin to work together with teachers on behalf of their children. By attaining level two, parents together with teachers can do so much for children, more than either party could alone (Pappano 2007). I believe children can feel when the principal adults in their lives get along and cooperate. For the child, continuity then exists between home and school, and a basis for progressing in the democratic life skills is established in the child's life.

In Study One, the teacher's happygrams and phone messages had a positive effect that was evident when Arlys attended the first conference. The transition for Arlys from level one to level two was shown during the conference. She and Mary Beth openly discussed the Pledge of Allegiance, holidays, and birthdays—topics that might have caused obstacles to their relationship. Mary Beth indicated that the two reached an understanding about these topics that sustained their growing partnership on Wilma's behalf.

Wilma was showing positive adjustment at school, experiencing no academic or behavioral problems. When children encounter a problem, the focus of the teacher and family member engaged at level two becomes how to work together to resolve the matter. The range of issues that can be addressed is broad, from extra help with school subjects to coordinated support for self-esteem to parental agreement for special education assessment and possible services. Cooperative engagement on behalf of the child indicates that family members have progressed to level two.

Teachers often know when parents have progressed to level two because they will take initiative to actively assist their child in the program. In Study Two, Cathryn agreed with Kay to have her son assessed for emotional challenges. When Cathryn agreed to have Curtis participate in special programming, she stayed in close contact with Curtis's teachers, "because I am the authority when it comes to my son and I know him best. We talk together about planning ways to deal with any problems he has." In my view, *all early childhood programs*, at a minimum, should have a goal of parent engagement at this second level.

Level Three: Active Program Participation

Families are engaged at level three when they participate in program activities in a way that goes beyond their own child. When family members reach level three, they take an active role that benefits the program, and the goal of establishing truly reciprocal interactions has been reached.

Commonly—though not necessarily—this kind of engagement involves volunteering in the setting. When family members first come into the room, teachers encourage them to take part in informal ways, like helping out and interacting informally with children.

When family members cannot be regular volunteers, the teacher and family work together in other ways, perhaps around gaining materials or services needed by the program or around participation on committees and at special events (Kersey and Masterson 2009). Parents ready to engage at a program level may be willing to sit on parent advisory and policy committees, and even to help represent the program to the public. Many working parents can build an occasional visit into their schedules—eating with a child during a lunch break or scheduling their work so they can go on a field trip.

In Study One, Mary Beth mentioned that she delayed having her kindergarten children learn the Pledge of Allegiance until spring. (Mary Beth did this at the suggestion of a veteran kindergarten teacher who one September heard a child proudly reciting, "I pledge Norwegians to the flag!") Mary Beth was pleased that Arlys accepted her invitation to share the family's beliefs about saluting the flag. When Arlys and the other two parents spoke with the class, all three showed engagement at level three.

Whether to do formal activities or just to visit, family members who come into the learning setting benefit their children greatly. A teacher once shared a story with me about an unemployed father who accompanied his daughter to preschool one day. He looked unsure as he entered the room, but the teacher welcomed him, introduced him to the children, and got him started reading stories. As he was reading, he overheard three children, including his daughter, talking about what their parents did. One child said his dad was a teacher. Another said her mom was a dentist. The man's daughter said with a smile, "My dad is here!"

In Study Two, through developing a trusting relationship with Kay, Cathryn progressed over time to being a leader in the weekly parent-child meetings, giving support and advice to newer parents. She also took the brave step to represent her local Head Start program at monthly Advisory Committee meetings, which meant a forty-mile one-way drive on very rural roads.

Level Four: Personal-Professional Development

For most early childhood programs, Level two engagement is a reasonable goal, hopefully for all families in the learning community. Level two marks the baseline for reciprocity in the parent-teacher relationship, the two functioning as a team to benefit the child. For other programs, teachers have a goal of level-three engagement for many if not most family members. Head Starts and later-generation comprehensive early childhood programs set level four as a goal for at least some parents. As a result of successful experiences at the first three levels, family members at level four engage in significant personal or professional development encouraged and inspired by the program.

Examples of such development are pursuing significant civic participation beyond the program (such as sitting on neighborhood, town, or county boards), furthering one's education, or progressing in a career. Additional schooling could mean getting a high school diploma, job training, or a bachelor's degree. The family member might become a teacher assistant or a child care provider, enter another field, or take on substantial new activities as an at-home parent. With support from a teacher, these parents choose to improve life circumstances for themselves and, by their example, for their families.

Level four engagement happens as a result of a family member feeling accepted by a teacher, taking more of an interest in his or her child's learning, and volunteering in the program. The parent gains so much as a person from the first three levels of engagement that he or she embarks on new paths for personal and professional development as a result.

In Study One, Arlys seemed to be engaged at level three and was progressing toward level four. She would be emerging at level four if, for example, she became an ongoing assistant to Mary Beth, or, in another direction, wrote a children's book about a child from a Jehovah's Witness family and her experiences at school.

In Study Two, I believe the thorough and intentional effort of Cathryn and Don to place their son in a small community school—rather than in a larger local school—indicates beginning level four engagement. Cathryn had to undergo substantial personal development to take the steps to advocate for her child outside the Head Start umbrella. Don and Kay's support were important, but the leadership Cathryn showed in this situation indicates to me she is progressing to level four.

In my university classes over the years, some of the most dedicated and responsive students have been parents who chose teaching careers after finding their niche by volunteering in early childhood programs. In these settings, teachers welcomed them warmly, helped them locate activities to do, thanked them for volunteering, and invited them back. Finding the experience exhilarating, the parents returned to these settings and became regular volunteers. They then made the decision and the commitment to become teachers. These parents ran the table, beginning at level one engagement and progressing through to level four. Significantly, when other family members see such accomplishments, it opens the door for them to engage in personal/professional development as well.

Two Teachers' Work with Families

Two kindergarten teachers from Minnesota, Pat Sanford and Sharon Hoverson, relate their approaches to building reciprocal relationships with family members.

Now retired, Pat Sanford taught kindergarten for many years in Bemidji, a college town in northern Minnesota. At one point in her career, Pat finished the coursework for a PhD but decided teaching kindergarten was more important to her than finishing her doctorate. The observations that Pat has shared with me over the years continue to be viable and informative.

 Pat takes a four-step approach to build relationships with parents and children at the beginning of the year. She begins by looking over contact information that parents have previously provided to the school. Pat says that rather than color her views, this information helps her begin thinking about the children who will be in her room.

1. A week or two before school starts, she mails a note to each child on Garfield the Cat stationery, saying how happy she is that the child is in her class. She tells the child to watch for the Garfield picture outside her room.

2. Pat also writes to the parents, introducing herself and giving some guidelines for her classroom to help the year start off right. In her parent letter, she includes her phone numbers and e-mail address. She mentions that she will call the children the day before school to get acquainted.

3. The day before school starts, Pat calls every child. She tells all of them again that she is happy to be their teacher and assures them that they will have a great time in her class. If she is unable to reach a child, she tries again, and continues to try other contact techniques, including home visits, with these few families after school starts.

4. Pat says the single most productive step she takes in building relationships each year is to call each family on the evening of the first day of school. She talks with the parents about any problems with bus rides, difficulties in the classroom, and so on, and she offers any needed reassurance.

Once when she learned that a child had a particularly difficult first day, Pat asked the parent if there was a jar of peanut butter in the house that the child could bring to school. "We could really use that peanut butter to put on crackers for snack," she said. The next morning the child proudly presented the peanut butter, and Pat expressed her appreciation—and felt relief when the child had a better day.

Pat shared with me that near the end of her career, she would have preferred to drink a beverage of her choice and hit the sack early on that first night of the school year. However, given the parent responsiveness that she saw over the early weeks each fall, Pat continued to make those annual calls. She says even now that those calls were an excellent investment of her time.

～ ⌒ ⌒

After volunteering in her son's kindergarten room, Sharon Hoverson returned to college as an older-than-average student and earned her prekindergarten/elementary teaching degree. She has since completed a master's degree in differentiated learning and has completed trainings in the many current curriculum programs, which she professionally notes keep spawning every year.

Sharon is a white teacher in Ponemah, a traditional village of the Red Lake Band of Ojibwe, where she has taught for almost twenty years. Sharon has the distinction of being the first teacher for the Red Lake Band to receive an Ojibwe name in a formal naming ceremony. She points out that the naming ceremony happened in part because a spiritual leader in Ponemah was an assistant in her room for many years. (That the esteemed elder returned to her class each year in itself says a lot.)

Ever since she began teaching for the Red Lake Ojibwe, Sharon has made home visits before and during the school year. Home visits were unusual for the teachers in Ponemah, most of whom were European American and, like Sharon, drove on and off the reservation each day. Sharon recognized that many families regarded the school as foreign territory. She always brought a teaching assistant from the community with her on the visits when she was just starting out, and she still sometimes does to this day.

During the first few years, the routine for the meetings was the same. In her well-used car (not a luxury model!), Sharon and the assistant would pull up outside the house. People in the house would look out to see who was there. The assistant, who knew everyone in the community, would get out and offer a greeting, often in Ojibwe. One or more family members would come out to the car, see Sharon, and ask, "Who's the blonde, white gal?" The assistant would say, "Oh, that's Sharon. She's your child's teacher. We go out and visit all the families before school starts. She wants to meet you and Rita (or Louella, or Darwin, or Virgil)." The family would bring the child out to the car, and Sharon would work her magic.

Sharon did many things in the community to show that she appreciated the families and the children. One year when a former student who volunteered in her class was tragically killed, Sharon attended the traditional burial ceremony. Present and past students flocked around her, and many families told her they were glad she had come. These days all the families with children in her class know Sharon and her car when she comes for a visit. They come right out to her, welcome her, and usually invite her in.

This chapter has looked at ways that teachers can make the ties to families that are so important for children a natural and accepted part of the encouraging learning environment. As children mature, there will be time enough for them to separate more fully from the family. While they are young, these connections should be celebrated so that each child feels a healthy sense of belonging at both home and school. By doing so, the child gains a foundation in DLS 1 (finding acceptance as a member of the group and as a worthy individual) and has a solid start on the other four democratic life skills.

Discussion Questions

An element of being an early childhood professional is respecting the children, parents, and educators with whom you are working by keeping identities private. In completing follow-up activities, please respect the privacy of all concerned.

1. Ask an older family member or acquaintance what they remember about their teachers' efforts to teach American values in school. (You might ask about hair and dress codes.) How are these practices similar to or different from what you experienced as a student? Discuss with others what you think the goals should be in schools today relative to socializing students for life in the United States.

2. Think about when you or children in your family or of an acquaintance were in school. Discuss a year when a teacher reached out to the family and worked to build a reciprocal relationship. How did family members regard the teacher? What difference do you think it made that the teacher worked to include your family in the education process?

3. Interview a family who is of minority status in your community because of linguistic, religious, racial, or cultural factors. Ask them about experiences they and their children have had relative to fitting into and getting along in the learning setting. Ask about the role of a teacher in being very/somewhat/or not very helpful in assisting the child and family to feel included in the learning community. Based on your experience with this family, what take-away learning can you share about the challenges faced by minority group families concerning their children's education? What do you think teachers can do to support families in overcoming these challenges?

Key Concepts

Definitions of the Key Concepts can be found in the glossary on pages 177–84.

Dual-language learners

Levels of family engagement

Melting Pot theory

Reciprocal relationships

Reflective listening

CHAPTER 5

Group Meetings:
Teaching for Life in a Democracy

FOR CENTURIES, ADULT COMMUNITIES around the world have held group meetings
to review past events, solve problems in the present, and plan for the future. Councils held by Native Americans, town meetings by New Englanders, and community
caucuses by political party members are examples.

William Glasser (1969) is credited with popularizing group meetings in American education for use with students. He called them *magic circles* and wrote popular works about the dual benefits of the meetings: teaching the group to respect
and appreciate each individual, and teaching each individual to respect and appreciate the group. Glasser viewed the meetings as essential preparation for life in
a modern, complex society—preparation he did not see happening in traditional
schooling practices.

In a modern application of the group meeting in the classroom, the widely used
Responsive Classroom model holds morning meetings as a staple (Kriete and Davis
2014). Kriete has written and updated the popular *Morning Meeting Book*, which
includes activities and ideas that build group spirit and assist children to understand that they are full and individually responsible members of the group.

The morning meeting component of Responsive Classroom recognizes a principle appreciated by virtually all adherents of these meetings in classrooms. Like
no other practice, group meetings give children real-life experience with the primary element of democracy: listening and talking in civil ways to cooperatively
resolve issues in manners that benefit all in the group. For writers ranging from
Dewey (1997) to Glasser (1969) to Hendrick (1992) to Vance and Weaver (2002) to
Kriete and Davis (2014) to Vance (2015), this prosocial aspect of democracy goes

This chapter builds on material from chapter 8 in *Education for a Civil Society: How Guidance Teaches Young
Children Democratic Life Skills*. Thanks to NAEYC for permission to adapt that material for this chapter.

| 89

beyond the competitive majority wins/minority loses political take common at too many levels of society.

In contrast to school councils, which include only a few from the entire student body, everyone participates in group meetings. While the teacher is the leader, she or he encourages friendly sharing and consensus building in relation to real-time matters facing the group each day. As with childhood art, the process is more important than the product for the children in the group.

 Head Start teacher TEAGAN: Today in group we are going to talk about our guideline "Friendly touches only." I wonder what *friendly touches only* means.

AUGUSTA: That we don't hit people.

TEAGAN: Thank you, Augusta. What do some others think?

TIMOTHY: Yeah, you can't grab 'em and push 'em.

WILLIAM: You can't do it if it hurts.

TEAGAN: So, we can't use our hands to hurt anyone?

KIKO: Or our feet either. Kicking really hurts!

TEAGAN (*smiles; she hadn't thought about kicking*): What can we do instead of using touches that hurt?

DANELDA: Use our words.

TEAGAN (*nods head*): Yeppido. I wonder what words we can use?

COUPLE OF KIDS (*Teagan has practiced this with them*): "This makes me upset!" "Teacher, help!"

TEAGAN: Yes, if you use words like these, I will come over and help us solve the problem. (*Pauses.*) Can we say, "You darn beebleberry?"

KIKO: Uhh-uhh, Teacher. No calling names!

TEAGAN: Oh, that's right; I forgot. But those other words are okay?

DANELDA: You know they are, Teacher.

TEAGAN (*smiles*): Say, I wonder what some friendly touches are.

SEVERAL KIDS: "High fives." "Low fives." "Fist bumps." "A hug if they say it is all right." "Patting on the back like you do, Miss Teagan." "Shaking hands."

TEAGAN (*smiling—and kidding*): "Oh dear, you all know so much about friendly touches! It makes me so happy, I think I am going to cry."

AUGUSTA (*looking puzzled*): "Yeah, we do, Teacher."

KIKO (*shaking his head*): "Why you gonna cry when you happy, Miss Teagan?"

TEAGAN (*now grinning*): "Thank you, everyone. You showed me you know all about friendly touches. Now it is work time. Sit here until you decide what you want to do. When you leave group, how about if you give me a high or low five, fist bump, hug because I say it's all right, pat on the back, or a handshake?" (*The kids sit for times ranging from half a second* [Kiko] *to almost a minute* [Danelda]. *As they individually leave group, they walk by Teagan and indicate which friendly touch they prefer.*)

Group Meetings with Young Children

Readers may wonder about group meetings at the preschool level. Polly Greenberg (1988) observed that meetings in preschools at the end of the day could review how things had gone and (if necessary) how things could be improved the following day.

In 1992 Joanne Hendrick advocated for regular meetings to teach the principles of democracy in the early years. She commented that group meetings can be of great value in "learning to trust in a group." Hendrick stated that "even four-year-olds can participate in making simple group decisions that solve social problems" (52–53).

Calling group meetings *community meetings* in a 1998 *Young Children* article, McClurg stated:

> The purpose of the community meeting is to create an intentional community devoted to a common project: learning to live with and take in the realities and perspectives of others. Here young children encounter and learn to acknowledge multiple realities, discover that they have choices, and realize that they are responsible for their decisions (30).

McClurg went on to point out that meetings help teach the skills of group living that adults want all children to learn:

> Some children may be too self-conscious; others may need to become more self-aware. Some may need to take control, while others are learning how to give. It is good news that, with a little leadership from an understanding adult, young children can learn these and many other things from each other. (30)

In 2002 NAEYC first released the important book *Class Meetings: Young Children Solving Problems Together* (Vance and Weaver). In 2015 the association published a revised edition as a featured comprehensive benefit book (Vance 2015). Along with the authors mentioned, I have written about meetings in each edition of my textbook (1994–2014). Two Guidance Matters columns (Gartrell 2006, 2012b) also address this topic. As readers can see, for many years early childhood writers have advocated for holding group meetings. In these polarized political times, more than ever, we need the civil influence of group meetings at all levels of education, beginning in early childhood.

Different Than Circle Times

Group meetings are different from circle times. Circle times generally address the routines of the early childhood classroom: opening activity, weather, calendar—sometimes with fingerplays, show-and-tell, songs, and stories thrown in. On occasion, circle times flow into group meetings and vice versa. But group meetings have a different focus, transcending daily rituals to deal with real life in the classroom.

A segue from circle times to group meetings might be special events, such as a new pet or a visit to the doctor, reported by any member of the group. Some children may share *a lot*. When this happens, teachers work with these children individually, perhaps arranging a personal schedule for the days when they can share in the group, with the assurance that they can talk with the teacher any day at a later time. Teachers also monitor for rough situations a child might be going through, talking with the child about what she or he might and might not like to share in group.

Group meetings are expressly designed for involvement by every child. Vance (2015) reiterates that their purpose is to encourage reflection and sharing by children and teachers about their experiences, needs, concerns, and triumphs to build a sense of acceptance of all in the group.

As Harris and Fuqua (2000) observed, when teachers keep group times concise and engaging, even young children become attentive participants. As open-ended activities do for developmentally appropriate practice, group meetings help define the encouraging early learning community.

Three Purposes for Group Meetings

Glasser (1969) identified three purposes for group meetings: open-ended group meetings, educational group meetings, and problem-solving group meetings. In my view, all three types fit most early learning settings.

1. Open-ended group meetings are for discussing hypothetical or real-life situations. Here is an example of how a teacher might begin an open-ended meeting with a group:

> "We have a new child joining us tomorrow. Melinda uses crutches to get around, like in the book we read. Teacher Kayla has brought in some crutches today so you can try them and see how they help Melinda. She is a very special kid—just like all of you. What ideas do you have for helping Melinda feel welcome in our group tomorrow?"

The vignette in the opening section, concerning friendly touches, also illustrates an open-ended group meeting. That meeting did not address a specific problem kids were having in the program but sought to teach the children about a guideline in the program. Open-ended group meetings can be considered almost group contact talks. Through talking and listening together, handled with care, members develop positive feelings toward themselves and each other. Friendly relations then thrive in the group.

2. Educational group meetings are for introducing, planning, and reviewing ideas, activities, and projects pertaining to the curriculum. For example:

> "Tomorrow, we are all going on our regular outdoor activity. We will hike and wheelchair outside to look for signs of spring. Cecelia [the assistant teacher] will write in our science log what you tell her you see. What are some guidelines you think we should use on our field trip?"

The following vignette, from my second year of teaching Head Start, illustrates the use of an educational group meeting.

Accepting that others see this matter differently, I have always had a problem with teacher-made bulletin boards. To me they are show-and-tell for teachers, quickly becoming part of the background and barely noticed by the children who walk by them each day. For adults who visit the learning setting, the bulletin boards are there, then gone.

Instead, participatory bulletin boards created by children and teachers together can become interactive visual symbols of the encouraging learning community. I came to this position in my second year of teaching Head Start. The class and I were getting into the holiday season. The holiday open house was coming at the end of the week, when family members would join the children and staff for a get-together. I looked at our now-dusty autumn-themed bulletin board and knew it had to be replaced. We had a group meeting.

DAN: Holiday season is coming and I need you all to help me with something. We need to make a holiday bulletin board for your families to see. Who has ideas about what we can do?

RITA (*no pause*): We can do "Night before Christmas." (*We had read the picture book.*)

DAN: That's a good idea, Rita, but how would we do that?

RITA: I can make the guy coming down the stairs.

JOEY (*pitches in*): I can make Santa. Where's that cotton, Dan?

CHEYENNE: I can make the chimmy that Santa comes out of with the socks.

KAREN: I can make the roof with the sled on it, but not the deers 'cause it's night and you can't see 'em.

Jodi or LORRAINE (*who did lots of things together*): We can make the tree, a big one.

DAN (*The younger two-and-a-half- and three-year-olds didn't say anything; I didn't want to put pressure on them*): Okay, everyone else can make anything they want for the "Night before Christmas." I will make the letters that tell adults what our bulletin board is about.

Everyone set to work. I was amazed at how intentionally busy the group was.

The youngest kids all went to one table. They got colored paper and markers. They cut out many small shapes. To some extent they appeared to be squares. They marked a single big crisscross on each shape.

DAN: Holy tamale, you guys are working hard!

ANTON: Makin' presents, Dan!

The kids each came to the bulletin board and told me where to place their contributions—it had to be the most creative "Night before Christmas" bulletin board ever! With the letters, the family members all recognized the theme of the bulletin board and were amazed by the representations the kids had come up with. The children showed family members which parts they had made. Big smiles all around. My moustache was permanently turned up at the corners that whole afternoon.

But that isn't the end of the story. In January, after break, I was getting ready to take down the bulletin board. The first bus came in. Rita asked me what I was doing. I explained it was a new year and we had to move on to other things.

RITA: Teacher, we made it. We will take it down.

I put a table underneath our too-high bulletin board. Rita and Virgil stood on the table, with me spotting. They carefully removed the pieces and handed them to me. I gave them to Jodi and Lorraine, who put them in a big portfolio. I kept the pieces for many years but unfortunately lost them in one of our moves. I will never forget what came out of our educational/real events group meeting.

3. Problem-solving group meetings are for discussing public conflicts when or shortly after they occur. A classic example of a problem-solving group meeting with preschoolers is from a state that gets some snow. It started like this:

"Today on the playground there was some hard snow wrestling. Some children got snow inside their clothes. They got cold and did not like it. Remember our guideline, 'Friendly touches only.' What can we do so we don't have this problem again?" (We will return to this group meeting shortly, but first . . .)

A Problem-Solving Meeting with Toddlers about Biting

Professionals I have known over the years insist that meetings with toddlers benefit children even at this age level. The clump technique tends to be used, with two or three kids sitting on or around each adult during the meeting. One of my favorite anecdotes is about a toddler group meeting in a Minneapolis child care center that addressed a challenging problem for adults and children alike: biting.

Toddlers bite for a combination of reasons, which often come down to wanting things for which they cannot yet express their desire in words. This serious mistaken behavior—that professionals dread having to explain to parents—can be an experimental mistaken behavior (level one) if done by a child only once or twice. But the strong reactions the child receives sometimes reinforce the behavior. The experimental mistaken behavior then devolves into socially influenced mistaken behavior (level two). This is often the case for the few toddlers who bite more than once or twice. In the toddler room of this center, Brian and Sam had gotten into the habit of biting a few of the younger toddlers, much to the alarm of the staff.

The staff met and discussed the matter with the director. They decided to try a toddler group meeting. The adults first explained the problem in simple terms. Then they taught these very young children this strategy: When a child approached in a menacing manner, the toddlers were to hold up their hand and say loudly, "Stop!" The teachers and children practiced together that day and the next. The following afternoon, when Brian came toward her with a grin on his face, Margareta held up her hand and said, "Stop!" The staff was over there in a flash. They prevented the imminent mistaken behavior and gave positive acknowledgment to Margareta.

Margareta and another child repeated the warning when approached again the day or two that followed. The teachers found that this response broke the impulse of the approaching child, alerted the teachers to get over to the situation for some quick problem solving, and helped children who might otherwise be victims to be rightfully assertive. With this strategy and accompanying guidance for all parties concerned (especially the children doing the biting), the problem lessened, to the relief of all.

In fact, Brian began pretending to threaten. When another toddler said stop, he would run away with a big grin. When a child firmly told Sam to stop, he actually began to cry—reminding the adults just how young these children were. (Compared to the biting, the teachers considered these reactions to be easier problems to work with.)

Agreements and Guidelines for Group Meetings

Whatever type of meeting, a few simple agreements assist adults in leading the meetings:

- Anyone can talk.

- Take turns and listen carefully.

- Be kind to our mates (which in many programs means not to identify individual children when discussing problems).

Establishing such agreements, and the reasons for them, may well be the subject of one or more early group meetings. Teachers use these discussions to engender a spirit of community within the group (Vance 2015). Teachers may ask: "Why do we need to take turns? To listen carefully?" Such discussions teach children about perspective taking and civil communication that hopefully extends beyond the meetings themselves.

In addition to agreements that the group makes, the teacher might have personal guidelines for group meetings such as the following:

- All ideas are appreciated.

- The dignity of individuals is protected.

- Individual situations might require private remedies.

- Situations are described, not judged.

- Feelings are stated as I-messages. (See "Express Anger Carefully" on page 110 for more information.)

- A course of action is agreed on, tried, and reviewed.

- Meetings are to solve problems, not create them.

In modern-day group meetings, just as in Glasser's magic circles, there are no wrong contributions. Every child can say what she or he thinks and feels without fear of correction. To monitor personal judgments during meetings, the teacher often uses reflective statements that affirm what a child has said or meant. Let's return to the snow-wrestling meeting to illustrate:

CHILD: I got snow down my back. It made me cold and mad!

TEACHER: You got snow down your back and it made you very uncomfortable [a new word for the day]. Good thing we got that snow out! Everyone, you know our guideline: "Friendly touches only." What can we do next time so this problem with snow wrestling doesn't happen again?

The children share ideas. When the discussion approaches its end, the teacher makes a point to include the children's ideas. The group seems to like one possible solution in particular. The teacher reflects it back to them: "So next time, kids can tumble down our snow mound if they want to. But they won't snow wrestle? Will this idea work for us? Yes? Then tomorrow, before we go out, you all can remind me of what we decided, okay?"

Supporting Participation

Teachers use nonverbal as well as verbal supports to nurture participation in group meetings. The basic tools of nonverbal support are nods and smiles. In my view, nodding (shaking your head up and down) should occur several times during each meeting. As for smiles, ten per meeting is my suggested minimum. Even more is a good goal.

Suggestion: When managing a meeting, if two children speak at once, nod and smile at the child whose turn it is. Hold a hand out just raised a little at the child whose turn is next. Then smile and nod at the second child. If children are raising hands for turns, don't just choose one. Say, "Rita, then Virgil, then Darren, then Lorraine," and try to remember the order (the kids will correct you). When you ensure an inclusive atmosphere toward all in the group, even quiet young children will find they have things to say.

The early childhood professional encourages children as much as possible to manage the discussion's flow. (Child leadership in a group meeting was illustrated by my Head Start children in the previous vignette.) This means holding back on the natural urge to dominate the meetings, which Teagan successfully did at the beginning of the chapter. (She also showed that occasional self-deprecating humor helps keep the meetings light.) Still, the teacher's job is to lead children toward ethical and intelligent solutions, always working for consensus and a happy ending to the extent possible.

In everyday American life, fear of public speaking is a widespread phobia. Giving children a supportive, positive environment in which to express their views—and listen to the views of others—provides a foundation for speaking in front of others that in my view can be long lasting. For the teacher, leading group meetings reinforces an understanding mental mind-set that helps keep interactions positive throughout the day.

Getting Meetings Going

Vance (2015) offers helpful advice for teachers ready to try group meetings with their children:

> To use class meetings effectively, make a commitment to allow time for regular class meetings to support positive changes in class and individual communication and problem-solving skills. I recommend using class meetings daily for at least three months to reach a level of comfort and skill in facilitating the meetings and to give the children time to become familiar with the routines and processes involved in the forum for classroom communication. This extended period of time provides enough opportunity to observe the effects of class meetings on the classroom climate and iterations. For class meetings as with all good classroom management programs, patience, commitment, and consistency nurture long-term results. (2)

Authors cited in this chapter differ on how often to hold the meetings, ranging from three short meetings a day to one half-hour meeting a week. At both the prekindergarten and primary-grade levels, I suggest two five- to fifteen-minute meetings a day, one after arrival (or breakfast when possible) and one just before going home. Teachers might also hold additional group meetings when unexpected events or conflicts dramatically affect the group.

Early-in-the-Day Meetings

Early meetings are usually more fully developed than afternoon and impromptu meetings. Topics for early meetings might include the following, among others.
Open-ended meetings:

- Introducing and revisiting guidelines—"Friendly touches only."

- Emotional literacy topics—"What makes people sad?"

- Beginning philosophy—"Should the rainbow fish give away its scales?"

- Human uniqueness topics—"Why do we say *firefighters* instead of *firemen*?"

Educational meetings:

- Introducing special themes, projects, and activities—"Because it is the start of fishing season, we are doing special things this week. One of them is minnows in the water table."

- Introducing special events and visitors—"Today Harold's brother, Brody, is going to come in and play his tuba for us. I wonder what a tuba is."

- Reviewing past themes, projects, activities, and events—"What are some things you learned from having minnows in our water table this week?"

Problem-solving meetings:

- Difficulties with guidelines—"How can we walk more quietly in the hall so we don't bother children in other classrooms?" (Guideline is "We walk very quietly in the hall.")

- Difficulties with level two mistaken behaviors—"Today I saw some children who felt sad when they were called names. How can we make this better?"

- Difficulties with level three mistaken behaviors that have gone public—"Clyde had a hard day, today. Some chairs got thrown, and some children got hurt. Clyde had to go home early with his dad. I think we need to talk about what happened, how you feel about it, and what we can do to help next time." (Care must be taken with these meetings. I talk about this more under the next heading.)

- Sad or wonderful events that affect members of the group—"Tomorrow [assistant teacher] Robert will be leaving us. He is going back to college to be a lead teacher just like me."

End-of-Day Meetings

Children and adults alike are generally pooped at the end of the day. End-of-day meetings serve as a transition from the group to the home. The meetings are to reinforce inclusive group spirit in the members. They are typically informal, held just before children begin leaving. Adults might refer to something that occurred that day and ask the children to talk about it. Or they might just ask children to share an experience from the day, something that stood out to them. Here are some examples:

- "What do you remember from our trip to the park today? How did we do with our guidelines? What is something you learned?"

- Individual children might share a gratifying experience: "Today me and Cheryl did that whole big puzzle. Nelson helped too, and we did it! Teacher took a picture for our scrapbook!"

- Individual sharing might also be about a guideline not followed (with the reminder of an agreement that individual children are not identified): "Kids wouldn't let me play with them in the store. I am upset. All the mates play together, right, Teacher?"

If there is not enough time and/or energy to resolve an issue in an afternoon meeting, teachers might carry identified problems over to the next morning meeting. The teacher wraps up the end-of-day meeting on a positive note, maybe singing a transition song so children can prepare to go home, or transitioning to a final work time as families arrive to pick up their children.

Special Meetings

The teacher can also call a special meeting if something eventful happens that needs immediate discussion. One example is when a child becomes seriously ill or hurt, and other children witnessed or know about the event. Another example is when children witness serious disruption and/or harm in the learning setting. Adults might be tempted to brush off children's questions in such situations. Instead, they can hold a special group meeting and allow children to express and work through their fears and concerns.

Special meetings can be a difficult call for early childhood professionals to make. They decide to hold the meeting if members of the learning community are bothered and upset. The reason for the meeting is to help children work through their worries and feel once again that the learning setting is safe and secure for everyone.

Group Meetings to Address
Level Two Mistaken Behavior

Level one experimentation mistaken behavior usually involves individual children. To avoid embarrassment, teachers use guidance talks as privately as possible with the child. An exception is if a child acting at level one corrals other children into a level two mistaken behavior—for example, getting them involved in snow wrestling or in chorus name-calling. In these cases, group meetings are often held to resolve the problems, but identities of all are protected. If needed, the teacher can follow up with individual children at another time. Sometimes new equipment and activities, not adequately planned for, can cause level two mistaken behavior—a new climber, for instance.

A prekindergarten teacher held an afternoon group meeting before going home. Mari explained to the group that some problems were happening on the climber (newly set up) and asked if some children could share about them.

One child said, "I got bumped on the top and I nearly falled off."

Another child said, "Somebody stepped on my fingers when I was climbing up."

A third child stated, "I was going down the slide and someone was coming up and I bumped him." (These children were following the guideline of not identifying other children during group meetings.)

Mari helped the children discuss the problem a bit more. Then she summarized, "We need to use the climber safely so no one gets hurt. I wonder who has ideas about how we can do this."

She wrote down the children's ideas, stating them positively as guidelines:

- We sit or crawl on the top and don't stand.

- Only one or two kids can be on the top at a time.

- We give kids room when they are climbing up.

- We go down the slide—except on Fridays!

Mari really liked this last suggestion because she wanted them to get more upper-body exercise. (Upper-body exercise is lacking in many programs.) The idea also increased the children's calendar literacy about Fridays.

Mari slowly read the guidelines back to the children. The children agreed that they would follow them. She ceremoniously posted them by the climber. For a few days, she or another adult stayed close to the climber and provided reminders about the guidelines. The children soon had them memorized, and they reminded each other of them, especially on Fridays.

The conventional discipline tactic of group punishment would have been to remove the climber for a week, a month, or permanently. I bet you remember group punishments. A few kids were involved in mistaken behavior—being noisy in the hall or rowdy on the playground—and your whole group got punished. You were probably upset with the teacher, who treated you with little respect—probably you weren't to blame. Also, you were upset with the children who got you in trouble, and they were probably mad at you in return. The punishment was probably embarrassing—walking up and down the hall three times in complete silence, staying in at recess for a few days, or writing a hundred times, "I will not. . . ."

Group punishments create a me-against-you climate in the setting, the exact opposite of what group meetings are about. Like other consequences in traditional discipline, they punish children for what they don't know instead of teaching them what they need to know.

Group meetings to resolve mistaken behaviors that have gone public are the guidance replacement for old-time group punishments. They give children practice at public speaking, strengthen children's abilities to resolve conflicts peaceably, and reinforce each child's standing as a responsible group member. They create a positive group identity, not *me against you*, but *all of us together*.

Group Meetings to Address Level-Three Mistaken Behavior

A basic guidance principle is that to avoid embarrassment, a teacher tries to keep interventions with children as private as possible. Real life, however, means the teacher must balance this principle with the right of the group to a sense of well-being. If a child is losing control with aggressive behaviors on a spectacular basis, meetings can serve to help children cope and to form group strategies to keep all safe in the future. The sad vignette that follows illustrates this situation.

Jeremy was suffering from toxic stress due to witnessing violence in his home and possibly experiencing it. He was attending a child care setting with an experienced and caring staff. The staff was collaborating with a social worker, but there were days when Jeremy just couldn't cope. His frequent meltdowns involved throwing things and hitting his hands, feet, and head against the floor.

One morning, while Jeremy was meeting with his social worker, the group had a special meeting. The two teachers explained to the children that Jeremy was having some bad problems that his family, the social worker, and the teachers were trying to help him with. They explained that Jeremy needed everyone to be understanding [a new word for the day] toward him. The children came up with some ideas about how they could be friendly to him. One child said, "We can leave Jeremy alone when he's feeling sad and mad."

The two teachers talked with the children about what they could do when Jeremy was having a difficult time. They decided together that Mary Jo would go with the children to another part of the room and find something quiet to do while Louise helped Jeremy calm down (if necessary using the passive bear hug). Everyone would leave Louise and Jeremy alone until Jeremy calmed down.

The group had to use this strategy more times than they wanted, but at least the teachers felt they were all doing their best for Jeremy and the group. Eventually, with the mother's permission, the adults got Jeremy enrolled in an early childhood special education setting. The boy left the program, but Mary Jo and Louise at least felt they accomplished something by giving Jeremy the best environment they could and by helping him get into a program where he could get more personalized assistance.

In a later meeting, the two teachers explained that Jeremy had gone to a new school where he could get extra special help. They thanked the children for their friendliness toward Jeremy while he was a part of their community. The children and teachers decided to make a large card with good messages for Jeremy. Together they took it to the post office and mailed it.

Through group meetings, even during difficult times, the encouraging community is sustained. In the terms of this book, the community as a whole was gaining practice with the democratic life skills. Jeremy was having profound difficulties with DLS 1 and 2:

1. Finding acceptance as a worthy member of the group and as an individual

2. Expressing strong emotions in nonhurting ways

Through the liberation teaching shown to him by the teachers, Jeremy was making whatever progress he could in this particular setting. When he could not respond, his teachers helped him find a placement where he could receive more focused assistance. While he was in the group, children and adults alike remained friendly to Jeremy. No one showed hurting behaviors toward him—they were able to take a more supportive perspective on Jeremy and his problems, aided in this process by the group meeting.

The group was making progress with DLS 3, 4, and 5:

3. Solving problems creatively—independently and in cooperation with others

4. Accepting unique human qualities in others

5. Thinking intelligently and ethically

Concluding Thoughts

As group meetings become established in the encouraging community, children come to value them. The teacher will know that community meetings are having an impact when children take more responsibility for running them and the teacher is (sometimes) able to sit back and watch (McClurg 1998).

> Over time, children will begin to care for one another, solve their own problems, feel more empowered and more in control of their learning, and come to view all in the community as their "teachers." It will be time well spent when the teacher sees what happens during [group meetings] coming around again and again. (Harris and Fuqua 2000, 47)

Some of the most important learning that the group and teacher will do occurs as a result of community meetings. As with all situations in which children are guided to express their feelings and thoughts civilly, group meetings teach children important lessons in social studies. The lessons center around how to see things as another does, and how to resolve conflicts in civil ways. Children practice high-level language arts communications as well, by gaining experience in expressing complicated perceptions and emotions in front of others, and by listening to and respecting what others are saying. Group meetings empower much-needed communication skills needed in further schooling and life beyond. In these ways and others, group meetings provide a solid foundation for learning the democratic life skills and, I believe, point to a direction that education at all levels needs to take.

Discussion Questions

An element of being an early childhood professional is respecting the children, parents, and educators with whom you are working by keeping identities private. In completing follow-up activities, please respect the privacy of all concerned.

1. Given what the chapter had to say about the value of group meetings, why do you think the practice is not more widely used in public and preschool programs?

2. Think about a group meeting in which you participated at any level of your education. Which of the three meeting types was it? Discuss how you felt about the outcome of the meeting and about your participation in the meeting.

3. For question 2 above, discuss how the teacher(s) facilitated the meeting—what went well and not so well. How would you have led the meeting if you were the teacher?

4. Select any one of the five democratic life skills. How do you think regular group meetings would help a child make progress toward gaining this skill?

Key Concepts

Definitions of the Key Concepts can be found in the glossary on pages 177–84.

Educational meetings

Group guidelines

Group meetings

Open-ended meetings

Problem-solving meetings

CHAPTER 6

Calming the Storm

Teacher-technicians typically react to dramatic conflicts by restoring order through traditional discipline—comforting the "victim" and punishing the "perp." In contrast, after triaging for physical harm, early childhood professionals who use guidance first calm all involved, beginning with themselves. After the time and sometimes space needed to cool down, the early childhood professional holds a guidance talk or mediation to resolve the issue and restore an encouraging climate in the learning setting.

Mental Outlook: Manage Your Emotions First

Why is it that, in the midst of spectacular classroom conflicts, some teachers are able to stay calm and others find it difficult to manage their emotions? "Calm everyone first, including yourself" is an important guideline. No one, adults or children, can resolve conflicts civilly when upset. Even in traditional discipline, a common instruction is "Never punish out of anger." The guidance equivalent is "Manage your emotions first, then calm and guide."

Let's face it: a proclivity in an adult for outrage or slow-burn anger, even when seemingly justified, is going to make life difficult for everyone in an early childhood setting. The same goes for unreliable impulse control and becoming easily upset when children's behaviors get challenging. When a teacher's challenging personal circumstances, or long-standing personality factors, are the cause of these behavior tendencies, she or he should do something about it.

Working out frustrations through physical activity can be an effective outlook builder—whether by going to a fitness center, running or swimming, or simply becoming more active during the program day. Yoga and other types of mind/body spiritual programs can also boost mental outlook. In terms of the basic needs of adults, you know the drill: eat right, get enough rest (a big factor), and keep solid ties with significant others.

At the talk-and-listen level, staff members who are friends can be invaluable. Outside the setting, so are family members and friends who will listen and be supportive. Counseling and therapy are also valid options; these are signs of strength in a professional, not weakness. The saying "You've got to take care of yourself in order to take care of children" is right and true. When personal circumstances outside the setting make things in the setting challenging, the teacher just plain needs to improve her or his personal support system.

Leaving It All at the Door

It is easy to say that early childhood professionals leave personal difficulties at the door. Nonetheless, many teachers do indeed experience an upward mood swing at their first interactions with children that day. And this is a good thing!

Teacher Glenda had been having dental problems for a week and was still waiting for her appointment. Her partner was out of town for a few days. One of her kids was having sleep issues, and Glenda was up with him for much of the night. It was a warm morning, and the door from the room to the outdoor play area was open for the children as they arrived. Glenda got to the center late and hurried into the classroom.

Hyacent, just four years old, raced into the classroom right after Glenda. Sporting a big grin, Hyacent ran in a circle around Glenda, came to a jumping stop in front of her, pointed to her feet, and said, "Me gots new 'letic shoes, Teacher!" Glenda knew that the girl had been needing new shoes for a while. She smiled, knelt down, and said. "I see you have new athletic shoes. They have lots of bright colors. I bet you can run very fast in them!" "Yup, I can. Watch me, Teacher!" And with that, Hyacent spun around and sped off to the playground. Glenda watched the girl run to all corners of the playground, stopping to show her new shoes to other adults. The teacher's smile got almost as big as Hyacent's.

The self-determined mental outlook of adults in early learning settings directly affects the challenge of staying calm. A 1987 *Young Children* article written by Nancy Weber-Schwartz remains clear on this matter. Out of respect for the author, with whom I agree, I will lay the argument out in her terms. Weber discusses the issue of patience versus understanding. My Microsoft Word dictionary definition for *patience*, just about identical to the one Weber-Schwartz used, is "the capacity to accept or tolerate delay, trouble, or suffering without getting angry or upset."

Weber-Schwartz's observation is that adults who rely on patience see the early learning setting as a place where there is often trouble that adults must keep from getting angry or upset about. Patient teachers are more likely to *tolerate* interactions in the setting rather than make the effort to understand and possibly even enjoy them. These adults may well stay distant in relations with children, whom they see as the ongoing potential source of troubles and suffering. In Weber-Schwartz's view, there will come a time when a child or a conflict causes the adult to lose patience. The child may then become an unconscious target. So much for the statement you often hear from people when they learn that you work with young children: "You must be so patient!"

For Weber-Schwartz, *understanding* is forming and keeping an open attitude toward others. Teachers can run out of patience but not out of understanding. She meant that the early childhood professional is understanding of young children in the here and now while also being open to fuller understanding of them into the future.

Let's use the preceding vignette with Glenda and Hyacent to illustrate. An adult who feels that her job is to be patient might have let her own suffering influence her reactions—and might have reached the out-of-patience point. An excited child running in the room might result in an admonishment for running and possibly for referring to the adult as "Teacher" rather than her proper name. Such a reaction would put a damper on Hyacent's pleasure about her new shoes and about sharing her feelings at school. Her trust in a significant adult in her life would diminish.

Instead, Glenda put aside her own situation, understood what the new shoes meant to Hyacent, and calmly celebrated the shoes with the child. Such shared quality moments lead to sustained trust and a closer bond between the two, whatever future interactions entail.

Once, in an early childhood education class, graduate student Rena (the teacher featured in my Guidance Matters column, "Aggression, the Prequel" [2011c]) disagreed with the way Weber and I define patience. Rena said that in her country of origin, Malaysia, patience is considered a noble quality, not the way Weber-Schwartz and I were characterizing it. Class time was up, so I asked everyone to think more about the matter and said that we would continue the discussion next time.

When the next class began, Rena raised her hand and said: "I have thought more about this. I think there is a difference between *enlightened patience* and *unenlightened patience.* When a teacher holds back when intervening because she understands the meaning of the situation for the child, that is enlightened patience. When a teacher does not understand the child, but holds back due to a need to be stoic, that is unenlightened patience."

Teacher Glenda held back on reminding Hyacent to improve her behavior. She did so because she understood the importance of the new shoes for the child. Do you think Rena would agree that this teacher was showing enlightened patience, a.k.a. understanding?

Express Anger Carefully

Imagine you see Marlon, a sixty-month-old, pry Sydney, a smaller fifty-month-old, off a trike, then get on it and speed off, running over Sydney's toes in the getaway. You comfort Sydney, triaging for injury, and walk over to where Marlon is watching. With a smile, Marlon says, "Sydney was done with the trike, so it was my turn."

Whatever the state of one's personal support system, once in a while any teacher may become justifiably—or at least understandably—angry, even when teaching young children. A leading educational psychologist of the 1970s, Haim Ginott (1993) contended that anger cannot always be controlled, but it can be managed:

> The realities of teaching—the overloaded classes, the endless demands, the sudden crises—make anger inevitable. Teachers need not apologize for their angry feelings. An effective teacher is neither a masochist nor a martyr. He does not play the role of a saint or act the part of an angel. . . . When angry, an enlightened teacher remains real. He describes what he sees, what he feels, what he expects. He attacks the problem, not the person. He knows that when angry, he is dealing with more elements than he can control. He protects himself and safeguards his students by using "I" messages. (72–73)

I-messages express strong feelings in relatively nonpunitive ways and focus children on the teacher's concerns. Ginott characterizes I-messages this way:

> "I am annoyed," "I am appalled," "I am furious" are safer statements than "You are a pest," "Look what you have done," "You are so stupid," "Who do you think you are?" (87)

Ginott suggests a *describe, express, and direct* practice for optimally using I-messages. This safeguard steers the teacher toward the problem rather than the child's personality. In the trike-stealing scenario, the teacher established physical proximity with Marlon, knelt down, and said:

Describe: "I know you thought it was your turn, Marlon, but it looked to me like you made Sydney get off the trike, and your wheel hurt your mate."

Express: "I am bothered by what I saw happen and that a child got hurt."

Direct: "We need to figure out a way to help Sydney feel better and for you to think what you can do next time so no one gets hurt. Let's talk about this."

I-messages are powerful. They should be used selectively, with discretion, and should not become an automatic part of a teacher's routine response. The careful expression of anger is not an end in itself, but a beginning point for implementing calming techniques and preparing those involved to talk through the conflict.

Directing comments to the situation and not to the personality of the child is an important guidance safeguard, one that Ginott called a *cardinal principle*. Ginott's position is that when teachers express displeasure but still observe the safeguards that protect self-esteem, children are more likely to listen and respond. I think highly of Haim Ginott and his ideas—so highly that I dedicated the sixth edition of my textbook to his memory.

Practices That Calm Young Children

Adults have difficulty resolving conflicts when their emotions are high. We cannot expect young children, with months rather than years of development, to have mastered this ability. Still, we can expect that children will make progress in learning the skill through our teaching and modeling.

Teachers know that when a child is too upset to talk, they must delay resolving the conflict and use calming practices first. Children who are very upset give the adult no choice but to help them calm down now and to talk later. In that moment, the strong feeling is what is real for the child. Anything else—such as explaining what happened or trying to minimize the child's strong emotions—will just add to everyone's frustrations. So, the question becomes, how do we help children calm down?

Reflective Listening

There are different terms for the most basic technique the adult uses; we will use *reflective listening*, the supportive acknowledgment of feelings. The technique calls for the adult to give nonjudgmental words to the emotions the child is showing and, in doing so, let the child know that the adult respects the child's feelings, and cares and understands. Here are two examples:

- "Sharlene, the tears are flowing down your cheeks, and you look very sad. Would you like to sit on my lap?"

- "You hurt your leg when you and Josiah were kicking. Let's just stay here for a few minutes so you can feel better. Then we'll talk about how to fix this problem."

A calming technique that is often used right after reflective listening is to have children take deep breaths, counting or breathing with them as they breathe (Gartrell 2014). A teacher who taught this technique reported seeing a child breathing deeply on his own. The child said to the teacher that if he didn't, he "would really get mad!" Counting to ten without deep breaths is another common technique used with older children. A teacher once relayed that she heard a six-year-old speed through the counting. She suggested that he still seemed upset and that he might try counting to twenty.

If a child declines the deep-breathing or counting suggestion, don't fight it. Direct the child to think of his or her own way to calm down and offer the gift of time. Remember that some children, particularly many boys, require more than a few moments to process events and settle their emotions (Pollack 2001). Children sometimes need more time to cool down than the teacher is first prepared to give. Separation in this case may be a helpful technique in the calming process. We call this a *cooling-down time*.

Cooling-Down Times—Not Time-Outs

A time-out occurs when a child is temporarily removed from a situation and placed alone in a separate part of the room with no alternative activity. Isolating a child in either a closed-off portion of the room or outside the room, unless in the company of an adult, is a harmful intervention technique not to be used (Copple and Bredekamp 2009). Over the years, the time-out has received criticism for being misused in early childhood settings (Gartrell 2014; Preuesse 2002; Readdick and Chapman 2000).

In a time-out, children are likely to internalize the shame of being separated, while simultaneously relishing the negative attention received from the teacher. This developmental reality means that periods of isolation fail to teach children how to get along better. Even when the time-out is considered a logical consequence by the teacher, the effect on the child is invariably punitive. Isolation diminishes self-esteem and generates negative feelings toward the teacher and the education environment (Readdick and Chapman 2000). In my view, time-outs contribute to the long-term stress-rejection cycle that guidance professionals work so hard to prevent.

A cooling-down time is different from a time-out (Gartrell 2014). In the traditional time-out, a teacher isolates the child in a quiet place in the room *as a consequence* of being in the conflict. The teacher typically asks the child to think about what the child has done. Preuesse (2002) points out that this request is developmentally inappropriate. By about age three, children can only just begin to understand the dynamics of situations—a capacity that takes until adulthood to fully develop. This is why the guidance of an adult is so important. Without assistance, children are likely to experience the time-out as highly stressful, internalize their anger and hurt feelings, and engage in a negative self-labeling process (Readdick and Chapman 2000).

When making the decision to remove a child from a group, the guidance professional asks and answers two difficult questions.

The first question is, Am I removing this child to cool down so we can talk later, or am I removing this child because of what he or she did? The truth is that sometimes teachers separate a child as a way of expressing their own anger. There are better responses to feeling anger than to temporarily expel a child, which is what a time-out is.

If the child is not upset, a more fitting response is to count to ten yourself and mediate the conflict (see chapters 7 and 8). A child who has hurt another typically does not want to hear from the other child and the teacher about the hurt she or he has caused. But level-headed mediation is exactly what the initiator needs to understand what happens when one asserts power over another (Galinsky 2010). The adult who can manage personal anger and resolve the conflict through mediation or a guidance talk has mastered a high-level guidance skill.

The second question is, Will the child calm down more easily if I am near, or will my proximity complicate the situation? The adult stays near a child to buffer against the punishing effect of separation and to calm the child so that mediation can occur. Children may find it comforting if they understand the adult is near to help them feel better. Sometimes, however, teachers know a child well enough to recognize a definite need for personal space as part of the calming process. A point worth repeating is that many boys and some girls need adequate "time and space" (Pollack 2001) to calm down. In this case, teachers get the child settled, give the child enough space, and facilitate the resolution later.

The following anecdote illustrates an appropriate use of separation to cool down—as distinct from the punishment of a time-out.

Eldar, aged thirty-nine months, joined Roget, forty-two months, at the playdough table. When two other children left, Roget amassed their quantities of the precious substance. Eldar did not ask, "I see you have a lot of playdough. Would you mind sharing some?" Roget did not say, "I have plenty of playdough. Take this generous portion." Instead, Eldar grabbed at the playdough bulging out from under Roget's left arm. Roget grabbed Eldar's wrist and squeezed it. Eldar screamed and used his free hand to start hitting Roget.

Teacher Darcy moved quickly to the table, separated the children and their chairs, and moved hers in between. Both children were very upset, and Darcy said, "I hear yelling and I see crying. We need to cool down, guys, so we can talk about this. Both of you take deep breaths." Darcy models; Eldar gets into it; Roget goes through the motions.

"Eldar, I need you to move your chair that way so you have more space. Roget, I need you to move your chair that way so you have more space." The two children know Darcy has helped them before, so they do what she asks. Between the deep breathing and the chair moving, the children calm down. Darcy then begins the steps of mediation (spelled out in chapter 7). She says, "Now that we are calmer, we are going to solve this problem. Please move your chairs back next to me. Roget, I need to hear what you think happened first. Then, Eldar, I need to hear from you. Roget first . . ."

If harm or serious disruption is occurring, adult leaders intervene. They triage for injury, help the children cool down, and use guidance talks and conflict mediation to resolve the problem and promote reconciliation. There are times, however, when the teacher must postpone the resolution part of the intervention. Either the children need more cool-down time than conditions permit, or there is too much else happening that the early childhood professional must attend to. Sometimes mediating later is actually more productive because the conflict has lost its immediacy for the children involved. Taking into account that professionals show positive leadership when conflicts occur, in resolving them time can be the teacher's friend.

Child Self-Removal

Early childhood professionals sometimes teach individual children *self-removal* to help them manage their emotions. Self-removal is only an intermediate objective in the long-term goal of teaching children to use nonhurting words. Still, self-removal is an important accomplishment for some children. Teachers know when a child is using self-removal effectively, and they mark it as progress with a child facing strong unmet needs.

 I remember a resourceful teacher named Nellie who was guiding a child to manage his anger issues. One day when I arrived at the center, Jason was standing with the teacher outside a closed side door, yelling into the wind. (On a calm day, Nellie would not have used this method of allowing Jason to vent. The boy would have been heard for blocks!)

Another day Jason left a conflict, walked over to the teacher, and said, "Nellie, I am so mad!" Nellie responded, "I can see you are, Jason. Thank you for coming and telling me. How about if you go into the restroom, close the door, and spit in the sink as long as you want." A few minutes later, emotions calmed, Jason walked out of the restroom and headed right for the water fountain. He was a dry little kid! After quickly cleaning the sink, the teacher complimented Jason for removing himself from the situation and handling his anger. She had a quiet guidance talk with him and helped him rejoin the group.

Teaching the child self-removal was not all the teacher and staff did to help Jason with his problems. From her relationship with the mother, Nellie knew that she and her husband had been fighting. Jason and his younger sister had witnessed violence in the family, and the father had begun going to Alcoholics Anonymous. The teacher worked hard to maintain relations with the mom and also communicate with the father (whom Nellie also knew). In the classroom, staff members spent quality time with Jason that included contact talks each day to build his trust and their relations with him. Over time Jason progressed in his ability to manage his anger.

Self-removal is only one part of a comprehensive guidance plan to help the child deal with unmanageable stress. Over time, teachers may notice a child beginning to use self-removal less as emotion management and more as a learned behavior to get out of everyday activities! If so, they should smile, because the child is progressing from level three mistaken behavior to level one. Guidance talks should continue, but the staff should also work to make involvement in activities more meaningful for the child. In Jason's case, the staff expressed the friendly expectation that he join in.

One now-established approach to the whole matter of self-removal—available to staff members as well as children—is to make one small corner of the classroom into a tropical island. The corner might have a carpet designated as sand with a ring of ocean around it; it might be equipped with a real or prop palm tree, a fuzzy stuffed sea animal, soft music, and sitting pillows. When children (or adults) are having a level three day and need to relax, they go to the island!

Teachers can give children the choice of the island or a chair in order to get calm, but they don't order children to the island. (The island is a place to cool down, not a pleasant location for a time-out.) Teachers also watch for children who go to the island on their own. Adults offer assistance to these little tourists in quiet and friendly ways. (If a staff member spends too much time on the island, an adult guidance talk—and maybe some time off—may be needed!)

On Restraining to Prevent Harm

Some children experience toxic stress levels in their lives and, as a result, show dramatic, level three mistaken behavior in the form of aggression. The emotional payoffs from aggression, including the adrenaline rush that comes from the conflict, can be reinforcing for a child. Teachers use firm but friendly words and actions to prevent the stress-rejection cycle. The very foundation of guidance is undermined if teachers allow any members of the encouraging community to harm or be harmed.

Two established systems for preventing and responding positively to serious childhood conflicts are the Crisis Prevention Institute and the Technical Assistance Center on Positive Behavioral Interventions and Supports.

1. The Crisis Prevention Institute (CPI) "is an international training organization committed to best practices and safe behavior management methods that focus on prevention." CPI provides a comprehensive system for creating a positive environment "and responding to conflicts with minimal-force restraint techniques that are appropriate, effective, and safe in situations where there is a threat of imminent harm" (CPI 2012). Not limited to classroom use, CPI provides "training and consulting in behavior management and dementia care." The website reports that "since 1980, over ten million

human service professionals around the world have participated in CPI training programs."

2. The Technical Assistance Center on Positive Behavioral Interventions and Supports (PBIS) advocates for and trains educators in a school-wide program to prevent and intervene positively with seriously aggressive and disruptive behaviors. PBIS, established by the U.S. Department of Education's Office of Special Education Programs, is a system that is available nationwide and is being used in over 21,550 schools.

According to their website, "Classroom PBIS includes preventative and responsive approaches that may be effectively implemented with all students in a classroom and intensified to support small groups or a few individual students. Classroom PBIS strategies are important tools to decrease disruptions, increase instructional time, and improve student social behavior and academic outcomes" (PBIS, accessed 2017). It is significant in PBIS that restraint and removal are last resorts, not to be used with common incidents of classroom disruption. The goal is to prevent serious outbursts, and if they do occur, not to unduly punish, but to use intervention methods that de-escalate conflicts and reduce the possibility of harm.

CPI and PBIS are both guidance-oriented systems that go well beyond traditional assertive discipline methods still used in many classrooms. More for use with older students, CPI and PBIS are helping educators learn to build positive environments and to cope in potentially violent situations. My understanding of these systems, however, is that neither has programs specifically designed for use with young children. The preliminary stage of young children's emotional and social development means that they may not pick up on the verbal and nonverbal cues that older children can. When young children lose emotional control, they lose it completely, kicking, biting, and throwing things. Training in the systems is no doubt beneficial for an early childhood professional in dealing with such behaviors. But when faced with a preschooler's full-scale outburst that is plainly causing harm, the teacher sometimes has to use the calming method of last resort, the *passive bear hug*.

Restraint and the Passive Bear Hug

The passive bear hug (PBH), used for years in early childhood programs, is the calming technique of *last resort*. Notably, it is *not* any of the notorious methods of not-so-subtle corporal punishment used on children in the past. This physical restraint is *not* paddling, spanking, slapping, ear pulling, hair yanking, back-of-the-neck squeezing, knuckle whacking, retribution child biting, mouth taping, or binding to a chair. Neither is it pushing or pulling a child, nor holding a child upside down!

Teachers use passive physical restraint when a child has lost control, physically and emotionally. A child in need of the PBH may be attacking another child, the teacher, or another adult. The child also may be causing self-harm by hitting body parts against a floor or wall. The PBH means holding a child so that his arms, legs, and head cannot harm you or himself. It is arms around arms, legs around legs, and going into a sitting position. The teacher holds the child facing away and at an angle to one side to prevent rear head butts.

Once the teacher decides that the PBH is necessary, the commitment is total. Children generally show survival behaviors, reacting strongly and negatively to physical restraint. This is not a fun technique for any early childhood professional, but the teacher stays with it, often speaking soothingly to the child. With many children, calm words, quiet singing, or rocking helps; other children calm down more easily with stillness. The passive bear hug provides limits that the child, for the moment, cannot provide for himself.

As the child comes to realize that the teacher is not trying to harm him but is providing needed structure, he calms down. Gradually, most children find the physical closeness comforting. Strange as it might seem, many teachers report that the PBH ends with the child snuggling against them. (Who needs a hug more at this point is an open question.) The teacher provides guidance if the child is able to talk about the event at the time, but usually a guidance talk happens later. After physical restraint, children (and adults) are drained. Helping the child into a quiet activity, such as reading a book, promotes reconciliation.

Lewis and Denise, both almost five, were painting on opposite sides of an easel. Lewis peeked around the side and painted some red on Denise's blue sky. Denise painted blue on Lewis's wrist. Lewis dropped his brush and pushed Denise down. Denise yelled and began to kick Lewis's ankles from the floor. Looking furious, Lewis was in the act of pouncing when teacher Kyle arrived and restrained Lewis by using the passive bear hug.

Lewis struggled to get loose until he realized that he couldn't. After a few minutes, with Kyle speaking soothingly to him, Lewis quieted down. Kyle helped Lewis wash off his arm, then tended to Denise, who was sitting on the floor watching. Kyle kept close to Lewis, spending some quality time with the child over the rest of the day. He later had a guidance talk with each child, and he let Lewis's mom know that Lewis had had a rough day but was doing better. In the days that followed, Kyle continued to observe Lewis and made an intentional effort to build relations with the child. He was relieved that over the next week, the few conflicts Lewis fell into were less dramatic than at the easel.

PBH Policy and Practice

Programs need to have written policies regarding the passive bear hug prior to its use. Perhaps another staff member must be present if PBH is used or a written report must be filed after each use of PBH. Policies, of course, need to be in compliance with state regulations regarding behavior management. A common suggestion is for programs to have a booklet of all major program policies, given to and gone over with families at the time of enrollment. A policy regarding PBH might be included in a broader section on the use of guidance by the program.

A follow-up self-check by the teacher later in the day makes sense: Did the teacher use a level of force necessary to prevent further harm and not cause more? Was either the child or teacher injured? Programs can have forms for reporting the use of PBH. Class meetings to allay concerns in classmates sometimes are appropriate in order to restore a sense of safety in the classroom. The adult who models and teaches democratic life skills as a part of the curriculum makes guidance more effective. The teacher must weigh the power of silence against the child's right to dignity in deciding whether to hold a class meeting.

Almost always, when PBH is used, the early childhood professional needs to follow up with *comprehensive guidance* (chapter 9) to intentionally guide the child toward stress management and the use of nonhurting alternative reactions in the face of conflicts. Communicating with parents always needs to be part of the plan.

Young children have only months of life experience, and they are sometimes living difficult lives. Any young child is entitled to lose it at least once during the program year. Calming children before helping them learn to manage their emotions is a crucial guidance step. When serious mistaken behavior continues over time, however, the single practice of helping children calm down is not enough. A comprehensive strategy for addressing level three mistaken behavior then becomes necessary.

Practice Reconciliation

Readers perhaps can remember when they were students and had a conflict with a teacher. On the other hand, if the following day the teacher acted as if nothing had happened, the reader probably recalls feeling relieved. If things never were the same in the classroom, the year probably seemed long indeed.

As group leaders, teachers need to model and practice the process of forgiveness. Under normal circumstances, children are resilient and bounce back. They also forgive easily, more easily than most adults. Because teachers are important in their lives, children want to be on friendly terms with them. This was the case with Lewis and Kyle. Kyle worked after the confrontation to restore his good relationship with Lewis. Early childhood professionals alone make things right again between themselves and a child. Still, as we have been saying, some children take a while to get over emotional upsets. It is better if we don't *force* apologies.

Fostering Apology

Have you ever been asked to apologize to someone before you were ready? Whether you did for the sake of appearances or didn't for the sake of principle, you probably experienced conflicted feelings. (I know I have.) The same holds true for children, although most kids have something going for them that most adults do not. Unless children have deep unmet security needs, as soon they have regained composure, they are often ready to make up and be friends. For young children, there is too much to do to waste time not getting along with people. In my experience, this is as true between children as it is true between children and adults.

Young children do not automatically know how and when to reconcile. Adults should never force children to apologize, even though a common expression in early childhood programs is "Now you go say you're sorry." If the apology is part of a punitive consequence of something one child has done to another, that apology is going to be conflicted, both for the giver and receiver. True reconciliation happens only when conflicts have been resolved in children's minds.

Chapter 7 on guidance talks and chapter 8 on conflict mediation provide tools for teachers to lead children in resolving conflicts and reconciling. For now, let us say this: After the conflict has been resolved and equilibrium has been restored, tell the child that the other child feels bad and has hurt feelings. Ask the child how they can help the other child feel better. Free of the threat of punishment, young children frequently come up with ideas like these:

- "We could kiss the owie."

- "We could put a wet towel on it."

- "I could say, 'Sorry. Will you still be my mate?'"

- "I could shake his hand and tell him I'm sorry."

- "I could ask her if she wants to play."

Sometimes children will not be ready to reconcile right away; they are still getting over the conflict. I suggested to my student teachers that at such times they say to the child, "I can see you are not ready yet. This is okay. When you are ready, maybe you can figure out a way to be mates again." One student teacher who had this happen wrote in her journal that she didn't think the kids would ever make up (and that my input on this was bogus). Later that day, Callie saw the two children playing together. She further wrote in her journal, "Thought I had you this time, Dan, but darned if those kids didn't make up."

When they reconcile on their own, children don't go in for ceremony. They just basically pick up where they left off.

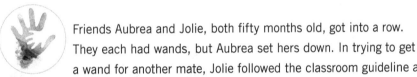 Friends Aubrea and Jolie, both fifty months old, got into a row. They each had wands, but Aubrea set hers down. In trying to get a wand for another mate, Jolie followed the classroom guideline a little too literally: "When you put something down, it means you are done with it." Aubrea chased Jolie out of the dramatic play area, clenched her fist, and told her, "I am never going to play with you ever again!" The teacher helped Aubrea settle down, reminded Aubrea of the guideline, and suggested that she make her own wand in just the color she wanted.

A half hour later, Aubrea and Jolie were playing an illuminated tile game together! Aubrea asked what color tiles Jolie wanted and gave them to her. Jolie let Aubrea decide where on the board to start placing their tiles. The two worked together in a most friendly way for the rest of the morning. The teacher made the reconciliation possible by using guidance to handle the conflict. On their own, the kids reconciled and became friends again.

Because Teachers Are Human

A challenge for all teachers is when they themselves have overreacted and crossed the boundary between firmness and harshness. Because expressing strong emotions in nonhurting ways is a high-level skill, even for experienced adults, teachers sometimes do cross the line. Perhaps a first step in recovering from overreaction is to acknowledge our feelings and forgive ourselves. Only then can we figure out how to make the best of the situation and reconcile with the other. Thoughts in the middle of the night may be part of this healing process, and talks with others important to us certainly are. Children sometimes *need* us to be firm. If we remember that the undercurrent of our firmness is appreciation of the worth of each individual child, reconciliation offers the possibility of fuller self-understanding and a more productive relationship.

Reconciliation is a matter of timing and inviting. Few are ready to apologize and make amends immediately after a confrontation. This is as true for adults as it is for children. Children, especially boys, may not be ready to reconcile with a teacher until they have had time to work through their feelings. (Children are ready to talk when they are not actively resisting the conversation.) After an adequate cool-down time, reconciliation often occurs with the follow-up guidance talk. Sometimes, though, children will take longer. Accept this reluctance and continue to model acceptance of the child.

With time, when the teacher invites reconciliation, children are apt to oblige. With young children, apologies and the acceptance of apologies are often expressed nonverbally. A hug can say "please forgive me" and "I forgive you" at once. In the encouraging learning community, teachers need to model that they too can learn from mistakes. True reconciliation means change. When teachers use guidance, change brings learning and growing each day.

Discussion Questions

An element of being an early childhood professional is respecting the children, parents, and educators with whom you are working by keeping identities private. In completing follow-up activities, please respect the privacy of all concerned.

1. Select a specific idea under the heading "Mental Outlook" that stands out to you as a take-away idea. Why did you select this idea? Share your thinking.

2. Select a specific idea under the heading "Practices That Calm Young Children" that stands out to you as a take-away idea. Why did you select this idea? Share your thinking.

3. Select a specific idea under the heading "On Restraining to Prevent Harm" that stands out to you as a take-away idea. Why did you select this idea? Share your thinking.

4. Select a specific idea under the heading "Practice Reconciliation" that stands out to you as a take-away idea. Why did you select this idea? Share your thinking.

Key Concepts

Definitions of the Key Concepts can be found in the glossary on pages 177–84.

Cardinal principle

Cooling-down time

Describe, express, direct

I-messages

Passive bear hug

Reconciliation

Reflective listening

Self-removal

CHAPTER 7

Teaching Young Children to Manage Conflicts through Guidance Talks

HEALTHY EMOTIONAL AND SOCIAL DEVELOPMENT in the early years gives children a psychological support system for cognitive learning at all levels to come. This is why teachers work hard to make learning experiences positive for young children. During the years when whole-child development is progressing at warp speed, early childhood professionals work to make learning experiences emotionally engaging. Teachers intentionally build programs that achieve cognitive learning, of course, but they rely on DAP and guidance to ensure that learning inspires—and does not turn children off to—further learning (Copple and Bredekamp 2009). In this way, teachers activate the most vital developmental dynamic for significant learning: intrinsic mastery motivation.

 For the first time Maxie, forty-nine months old, is trying the smaller Legos instead of the larger Duplo blocks. She is "making the house where Spiderman lives," and she is having trouble with a wall. Maxie wants to put a window in it, but she can't get the pieces right. Maxie crunches up her building, puts her head down on the table, and loudly says, "Damn!"

Recognizing this is a level one experimentation mistaken behavior, Sharlene sits down next to the child and says, "You having a hard time, Maxie?"

With her head still down, Max says, "That damn window won't go in!"

Sharlene rubs her shoulders for a bit. "I wonder what you could do to have a better time building?" (Pause.) "Maybe you could make the house out of the big bricks and use the little bricks for a table and chairs for Spiderman."

After a bit, Maxie sits up and says, "Yeah, and a bed even."

Sharlene adds, "Remember about that word, though. It bothers people in child care." Maxie makes a face but nods her head. Sharlene asks, "What could you say next time instead?"

Maxie grins at Sharlene and replies, "This is damn hard!"

Sharlene shakes her head no with a mostly solemn teacher expression. "Try that one again, Maxie."

Maxie says, "This is hard!"

Sharlene smiles. "That will work, buddy girl. If you say the words loud, I will come over and see if you want me to help."

"Okay, Teacher." Maxie gathers the Duplos.

To keep learning positive, even in conflict situations, guidance means teaching to children's strengths. Maxie's use of the expletive caused a conflict because the word made others (in this case Sharlene) uncomfortable. Sharlene still gave Maxie emotional support; at the same time, she coached the child to work on her wording. Sharlene used a classic *guidance talk* with Maxie.

Guidance talks come down to taking perspective and *scaffolding*. This dual operation means seeking to understand the child's viewpoint of the situation and, through interaction, quietly guiding the child to learn what she or he can at the moment about solving problems in the future. Referring to the vignette, Sharlene saw that Maxie became frustrated because she could not complete her task. The teacher empathized with Maxie about her frustration. Then she scaffolded with Maxie to make her stress manageable by suggesting an alternative approach. Sharlene did address the mistaken word, but by keeping the plastic bricks in play, she supported the child's mastery motivation through the activity. This is likely why Maxie immediately accepted the solution.

Why Young Children Need Guidance Talks

Life has its own special problems that months-old humans must deal with each day, problems relating to various combinations of the following:

- rapid-but-still-early brain development

- dependency on others for meeting many needs

- limited social experience, especially outside the family

- still-developing eye-hand coordination that can make seemingly easy tasks frustrating

- patterns of brain development that can lead to atypical learning behaviors

- challenging life experiences outside (and sometimes inside) the learning setting

- high susceptibility to stress and its effects

In any combination, the above stressors can make everyday situations challenging for young children. Maxie's frustration when she tried to use the smaller bricks for the first time is an example.

As Maslow maintained, children feel most strongly the basic motivation to attain safety and security. Only as these needs are being met can they respond productively to the second motivational set for learning and psychological growth. The job of early childhood professionals then is twofold: to assist children however we can to meet their stress-driven needs for safety and security, and, *at the same time*, to nudge them toward meeting their executive-function needs for learning and growth (Cairone and Mackrain 2012). Early childhood professionals take this two-part mind-set into all transactions with children, including, as in Maxie's case, when children experience conflicts.

Being Only Months Old . . .

In a still highly respected work in the field, Carlsson-Paige and Levin (1992) framed the developmental factor in teaching social problem solving this way:

> [Young children] tend to see problems in the immediate moment and in physical terms. They also see problems from their own point of view. Only with age and experience do children slowly learn to see problems in a larger context; in more abstract terms that involve underlying motives, feelings,

and intentions; and from more than their own point of view. Until they are able to do this on their own, therefore, the teacher needs to help. (7)

In our terms, because children are developmentally and experientially young, they need guidance talks to learn social problem solving and gain the skills they need to flourish in modern, complex society. Guidance talks give children a start in this vital learning process.

Conflicts over Property, Territory, and Privilege

Dinwiddie's (1994) concrete analysis of why young children have conflicts further explains Carlsson-Paige and Levin's observation. In a classic *Young Children* article, Dinwiddie stated that young children generally have conflicts over property, territory, and privilege.

Property tends to be the most frequent source of conflict in the preprimary years and the kind of dispute adults most often have to mediate. As teachers know, the concepts of sharing and taking turns are not natural ones for very young children. Two kids arriving at a tricycle at the same time is an example.

As children begin to play in groups, problems of *territory* arise. In some ways, territorial disputes seem easier to mediate than property disputes because sharing space is more easily negotiable than is a single object. However, a child already in an area often defines space needs quite differently than the other child or the adult. An illustration is this:

 Collin, a twenty-eight-month-old, is washing a plastic baby orca in a water table. A second child, Janeen, brings a Dora figure next to Collin, where there are two bottles of diluted, no-tears shampoo. Collin starts to scream and push her away. Teacher Amber arrives and tries to reason with Collin about how there is room for Janeen next to him. Through tears, Collin points to the other end of the water table and says, "There." Amber realizes that this not a deal breaker for play at the water table. She says to the second child, "Janeen, here is a bottle of shampoo. You will have lots of room to give Dora a bath over here. Is that all right?" Janeen nods. (She doesn't want a conflict; she just wants to give Dora a bath.) The two wash their figures until Collin leaves. Two other children come over, and Amber gets them started. These two wash plastic figures side by side and space is not a problem.

In territorial mediation, the adult frequently has to work hard to see the issue as the child does and sometimes literally has to give a bit of ground in mediations.

Early childhood professionals look at this situation not as indulging children, but as education for nascent negotiators as they begin to gain mediation skills. Another time, Collin might be the child to arrive second.

Dinwiddie observes that problems of *privilege* emerge as children's awareness of social subtleties continues to grow. Privilege conflicts, such as who gets to line up first and who gets to play with whom, are seen in older preschoolers and, as readers know, especially in older children! Children's increased awareness of social status can make mediation of privilege-based conflicts difficult. Guidelines set in class meetings beforehand can help as mediation points in all three sources of conflict, particularly in conflicts of privilege. "In our class, we work and play together" provides positive wording for the classic rule "You can't say you can't play."

In relation to lining up, a helpful practice is to use a list to determine who is leader (and, if desired, who is the caboose). The list might be based on age, height, or the letters of first names. Moving a marker down one side and up the other indicates, the turn for the two prestigious positions.

Young children have the conflicts Dinwiddie writes about at any of the three levels of mistaken behavior. Predictably, children at level three bring the anxiety of unmet basic needs into the conflict, ratcheting up the crisis factor in ways that children at levels two and one typically do not. This vignette is a conflict over privilege, or lack of, from the perspective of a forty-month-old who sees things only in the *right now*.

 Gabe was about to read to his family group. He was introducing the title and author of the timeless 1942 book *Make Way for the Ducklings* by Robert McCloskey. Gunnar, forty months old, got tired of the introduction. "Turn the page!" he screamed, and he took a swipe at Gabe, hitting him on the leg! Assistant teacher Marsha arrived from clearing the tables and sat next to Gunnar, putting her arm around him. He crawled on her lap. Gabe knew Gunnar well and whispered to him, "Now we can start."

The other children were used to Gunnar's outbursts and quick recoveries; they sat patiently. Gabe read the book, giving each of the ducklings the name of a child in the family group, to giggles and smiles. He called the first duck "Gunnar."

After story time, Gunnar was doing a puzzle. Gabe sat next to him and waited until he finished. Gabe said, "You really got upset when we were reading the book."

GUNNAR: You didn't turn the page.

GABE: But you are feeling better now?

GUNNAR: Yeah, Marsha came, and you read about the ducks.

GABE: That was a fun book, wasn't it? We called the first duck "Gunnar." (*The boy smiles. Gabe pauses.*) Gunnar, hitting hurts. Remember what to do next time instead?

GUNNAR: Say, "I'm sorry."

GABE (*quietly*): Listen to me, Gunnar. Use words, not hitting. Now you say it.

GUNNAR: Use words, not hitting.

GABE: You got it. You could say, "Turn the page, please." I would listen if you told me that. (*Pauses while Gunnar takes this in.*) It got better when Marsha got there, didn't it?

GUNNAR: Yep, we read the ducks book. Marsha's my mate.

Gabe used a compliment sandwich to make his guidance talk work. Triple-decker compliment sandwiches work best: two positives, then the clear reminder about a guideline that needs to be met, and then another positive.

First positive: By acknowledging Gunnar's feelings, Gabe was showing that he understood the boy and wanted to support him.

Second positive: Gabe prompted Gunnar to say how the boy saw the problem and helped him recognize the problem had a gratifying conclusion. (Notice no judgments on Gabe's part.)

Guideline reminder: Gabe knew Gunnar well and had him repeat what the boy needed to do next time. He also suggested to Gunnar words the boy could say.

Third positive: Gabe and Gunnar talked about how the rest of the experience was fun for Gabe, especially when assistant teacher Marsha came and sat by him.

At least a three-to-one ratio is important to make compliment sandwiches work, especially with kids who face challenges. The use of compliment sandwiches reminds both child and adult that the adult is on the child's side. They are working together to solve the problem so the child feels worthwhile as an individual and as a member of the group, and so he continues learning to express strong emotions in nonhurting ways. The adult leads, but in friendly ways.

Inside Guidance Talks

When one or two children have a conflict with an adult in the program, the early childhood professional intervenes with a guidance talk (GT). A guidance talk is not a public reprimand. It is not an opportunity for the adult to explain how the child was wrong and why the child should apologize. GTs are different from the age-old "lecture."

A guidance talk is talking *with* the child, not *at* the child. It is a teaching and learning opportunity for the child, and often also for the early childhood professional. One reason is that, like all guidance practices, GTs protect the young person's dignity. The talks sustain the proactively positive relationship that the adult is building with each member of the encouraging community. The GT asks the adult to

- start with calming techniques, which will reduce the likelihood of overreaction by the adult and/or child;

- listen to the child so that the adult is talking with and not at him;

- help the child to give her viewpoint as to what happened; and

- work for a resolution that helps the child (1) more fully understand what happened, (2) learn about nonhurting responses for when a similar conflict arises next time, and (3) reconcile with the other child.

Guidance talks are not wimpy. They are firm when they need to be, but firm and friendly, not firm and harsh. When GTs happen, consequences for the conflict are being imposed—for the child but also for the adult. For the child, the consequences are stated in the last bullet above. The consequence for the adult is to proactively assist the child to meet needs for safety and security and, at the same time, to nudge the child toward psychological growth. The early childhood professional does so by respecting the child's viewpoint and protecting the child's dignity. She or he teaches what the child is able to learn in that moment about how to handle future conflicts in nonhurting ways and about the importance of reconciliation. By the end of the GT, the teacher makes the expectation clear that the child needs to work on these skills.

A current trademarked technique for helping children to manage their emotions is FLIP IT, developed by the Devereux Center for Resilient Children (www.centerforresilientchildren.org/flip-it/). FLIP IT includes these four steps to managing emotions and learning social problem solving:

- Identify **Feelings**.

- Set or remind the child of the **Limit**.

- Ask questions—**Inquire**.

- Offer **Prompts**.

For example:

F: "I see you are angry."

L: "But we only use our hands in kind ways."

I: "What is another way you could ask for a turn?"

P: "You could ask your friend how much longer they will use the toy. We can make this work by setting a timer." (Sperry 2011)

FLIP IT is quite similar to the GT procedure, as long as readers keep in mind compliment sandwich considerations—just as they should with the GT. By this I mean using positive remarks during the acknowledgment and calming of strong feelings, such as "You were working hard on that. No wonder you are upset." These opening comments tell children that the adult is working with and not against them. Also toward the end of the process, the teacher does well to positively recognize children's efforts in solving the problem, reaffirming the teacher's faith in their abilities. FLIP IT is a quick, effective improvement on comparable traditional discipline interventions and definitely qualifies as guidance.

The purpose of the guidance talk is to use the conflict situation to teach children to manage their emotions in nonhurting ways. I use the term *manage* rather than *regulate* or *control* because for me (as well as Ginott), emotions exist in and of themselves, interconnected with, but not controlled by, cognitive processing. I don't believe that one can cognitively regulate emotions in the long run in sustainably healthy ways. It seems to me that productive human functioning is more a matter of balancing the emotional and cognitive dimensions of living, and using both processes together to reprogram potentially harmful reactions during conflicts into nonhurting ones. Manage more than regulate or control.

Guidance Talks and the Levels of Mistaken Behavior

Teachers use guidance talks with individual children who are involved in conflicts at any of the three levels of mistaken behavior. At level one, a child unintentionally or intentionally has tried an action that has upset or harmed another. At level two, a child has fallen into a conflict as a result of influence by one or more others outside or inside of the learning setting. At level three, a child is reacting to unmanageable stress and showing aggression impulsively or instrumentally—in either case a mistaken survival behavior gone wrong. Teachers use *perspective taking* to assess which level of mistaken behavior is likely involved before and as they engage in the contact talk with the child.

Level One Mistaken Behavior

A mound in the play yard becomes a chance for Denton to play king of the hill. Being the biggest kid, Denton pushes and bumps others off the mound when they run up to the top. Some of the older preschoolers join the game, but they all get pushed back down. Nicky, a younger preschooler oblivious to the roughhousing, comes up the backside of the mound. Denton turns around recklessly. Nicky gets bumped hard, falls down, and starts to cry. Teacher Paula has Denton come off the hill and sit down while she tends to Nicky. Paula uses reflective listening to help Nicky feel better. Then Paula and Denton have a guidance talk.

Denton looks embarrassed and upset at being removed from the game. Paula sits with him for a minute or two. Then she softly asks him, "Do you know why we are here talking?"

DENTON: We were just having fun.

PAULA: I think we call that game king of the hill. Looked like you were really being the king.

DENTON: Yep. Nobody could stay up there but me.

PAULA: Denton, you are the biggest kid. Nobody could get you off that hill! (*Pause*). But Denton, when you push and bump, other kids can get hurt, like Nicky. How can we play on the mound so no one gets hurt?

DENTON: We can give friendly pushes.

PAULA: You are really thinking here. But you know kids like Nicky could still get hurt. So let's think some more. (*Both pause.*) How about if you run up one side and tumble down the other?

DENTON: (*Pause while Denton processes this idea.*) Okay. The tumblin' is the fun part.

PAULA: That sounds like a plan. We would just have to give kids room. I will stay here for a while and remind them. I think Nicky is still hurting a bit. Can you think of a way to help her feel better?

DENTON: Go tell her I'm sorry.

PAULA: You really worked this out with me, Denton. Thank you.

DENTON: (*On his way over to Nicky*) You go by the hill so we can tumble, okay Paula?

PAULA: (*Grinning*) Okay. (*She knew that Denton would explain the new game to the other kids and that they would join in.*)

This clearly was a guidance talk with an older, verbal preschooler who had fallen into level one experimentation mistaken behavior. Denton's experiment of playing king of the hill (informally organized conflict play, over territory and privilege) simply got out of hand. Paula used a guidance talk in a way that worked for Denton. She complimented him as being the biggest kid and the king of the hill. She complimented his thinking as he attempted to solve the problem. With her prompts, Denton found a solution that would work for both him and Paula, and he figured out a way to help Nicky feel better. At the same time, Paula guided Denton to a solution that was in line with the guidelines for the group.

The other children who were following Denton in the game were engaging in level two socially influenced mistaken behavior. Perhaps the next day, the king of the hill lesson could be reinforced in a group meeting. Without singling out either Denton or Nicky, the group might discuss again what "friendly touches only" means when children are outside. They might talk about individual tumbling as an alternative. In guidance, teachers occasionally do just say no by setting a firm limit. But guidance professionals don't stop with just the "no." They teach for mutually acceptable, brain- and body-building alternatives.

Level Two Mistaken Behavior

Shelby's older brothers and sisters all were using the phrase "freakin'" at home. A cool television show was "freakin' good." A flat tire on her oldest brother's car was "a freakin' pain." Shelby, sixty-two months, stood up for herself at home and was a leader in the classroom. She soon began using the term just as her siblings did. One day Shelby hears Keenan (fifty-nine months) say, "This is a freakin' cool car." Shelby grins and says, "You said freakin' freakin'!" The teacher in charge of their family group quietly gathers the two children away from the others and sits on the floor with them.

Elin says, "It is cool to try new words, guys, but *freakin'* is not a word to use at school." Shelby says, "But you just said it, Teacher." Grinning, Elin replies, "Yeah, Shelby, I used it so you know what word I mean. Have you heard me use it other times?" Shelby shakes her head no. Elin says, "So let's think of some words you both could use instead. You could say 'really,' like, 'This is a really cool car.'" (There is a pause as the two kids look at each other.) Keenan says, "Teacher, I *really* want to go play with my car now."

Shelby rolls her eyes (a response she learned from an older sister). Elin says, "Okay, you got the message, right?" Both kids nod and are off. For the rest of the week Elin listens for, but does not hear, the word—in her view, ~~a freakin'~~ "really" an improvement.

Elin used a guidance talk with two children here. She did this to head off a potentially contagious level two behavior spreading to others in the group. She recognized that for both children this was mistaken behavior at level two. Shelby learned the word from siblings and repeated it at child care. Keenan learned the word from Shelby and repeated it. Teacher Elin made an effort to be firm but friendly during the GT. She avoided a moralistic lecture and simply established a limit regarding the use of the word in the program. This intervention was a guidance talk rather than a mediation because the two children were not in conflict with each other. This was an expression used by two children that happened to bother the teacher.

Level Three Mistaken Behavior

Guidance talks with individual children, of course, are frequently more challenging than the above illustration. When a child brings level three issues to a conflict, it is crucial that the early childhood professional already have an ongoing relationship with the child. If, after the conflict, the child sees the adult as making things better, the relationship building has taken hold.

Provider Andra can tell that Riko, forty months old, has already had a rough morning. An older sibling dropped Riko off late, and he came in with his shoes in his hands and tears on his cheek. It wasn't the first time Riko had arrived this way.

After breakfast, Riko and Marie, fifty-five months old, are at the sensory table, today filled with water and a variety of kitchen utensils. Usually Riko finds this activity soothing, which Andra hopes will be the case this morning. Andra sees Marie accidentally drop a pot of water, which splashes up on Riko. Riko loses it, throws water from a cup at Marie, and starts to cry loudly. The provider brings a towel and helps Marie dry off. The provider has another towel for Riko, and she leads him to a quiet place where they sit down. Andra dries Riko off, telling him that getting wet like that is no fun! Riko settles down, and the two have a guidance talk.

ANDRA: You got some water spilled on you, and you didn't like it, did you, Riko?

Riko shakes his head and looks down.

ANDRA: That pot was too slippery for Marie, and she dropped it.

RIKO: She got water on me!

ANDRA: Yes she did, but it was an accident. She didn't mean to.

Riko continues to look down.

ANDRA: She got a lot of water on her front.

RIKO: Didn't mean to.

ANDRA: You were sad and mad, weren't you?

RIKO: Yeah.

ANDRA: Marie is dry now. Can you think of a way to help her feel better?

Riko shakes his head no.

ANDRA: That's okay; maybe you can later.

Andra and Riko sit together for a few minutes. Riko gets up and goes to the reading corner where Marie is looking at a book. Riko gets another book, sits down beside her, and reads it. Marie does not object. (Thank you, Marie!)

Later Andra and Riko discuss what he can do next time if he gets water spilled on him—which Riko repeats back to Andra, "Get you, Teacher." Sometimes kids (as well as teachers) just plain have *level three days*.

Guidance talks depend on teachers who, from the first contact with a child, have worked to build proactive positive relationships. As with any guidance technique, guidance talks don't have to be done perfectly. For example, sometimes teachers must delay the problem-solving part of the guidance talk due to other pressing duties. As long as the early childhood professional acts as a guidance leader and not judge and jury, good enough is almost always good enough. When conflicts happen that equally involve two children or a small group of children, the teacher uses, models, and teaches conflict management, the subject of the next chapter.

Discussion Questions

An element of being an early childhood professional is respecting the children, parents, and educators with whom you are working by keeping identities private. In completing follow-up activities, please respect the privacy of all concerned.

1. Recall a conflict in an early childhood setting where you think the level of mistaken behavior was at level one, level two, or level three. In a nonjudgmental way, share what the conflict dynamics were that make you think it was mainly due to that level of mistaken behavior. If you think different children were showing different levels of mistaken behavior, share about that.

2. Recall a conflict in an early childhood setting where you think the main source of the conflict was a dispute over property, territory, or privilege. In a

nonjudgmental way, share what the conflict dynamics were that make you think it was mainly due to that source of conflict. If you think different children were showing a combination of the conflict sources, share about that.

3. Think about and share the differences you see between an adult intervention with a child that is the traditional discipline technique of lecturing and one that is a guidance talk. What might be the consequences of each for the child? For the teacher?

4. What are your thoughts about the author's view that guidance talks don't have to be done perfectly, just good enough? How can you tell if a guidance talk is good enough for the child? For the adult?

Key Concepts

Definitions of the Key Concepts can be found in the glossary on pages 177–84.

Compliment sandwich	**Privilege conflict**
Guidance talk	**Property conflict**
Level three day	**Scaffolding**
Perspective taking	**Territory conflict**

CHAPTER 8

Teaching Young Children to Manage Conflicts through Mediation

LET'S BEGIN BY DEFINING some terms you'll find in this chapter:

Conflict management: The ability to de-escalate and resolve conflicts through the use of nonhurting words. The composite abilities of DLS 3, 4, and 5 applied in conflict situations that we want children (all humans?) to learn to use.

Conflict mediation: During an escalating conflict, the method used by a third party, usually but not necessarily an adult, to teach the children involved to de-escalate and resolve the conflict in nonhurting ways. (In my guidance approach, the method we use is the *five-finger formula*; discussion to follow.)

Peer negotiation: The process whereby two or three children by themselves de-escalate and resolve a conflict peaceably; evidence that children have achieved a key guidance goal by using the basics of conflict management without the help of an outside party.

Social problem solving: The generalized ability to resolve issues and problems through proactive, civil interaction; making intelligent and ethical decisions within the context of a group. Includes, but is broader than, conflict management in that it addresses issues and problems from even before a conflict starts.

Inside Conflict Management

As you may have gathered, I write in terms of philosophical as well as psychological child development. Based on my fifty years of studying the issue and my contacts with early childhood professionals in a host of settings, my position is that with caring guidance young children are able to act ethically and intelligently to resolve conflicts.

Guidance professionals regularly observe young children (such as Jeremiah resolving the truck dispute in chapter 2 and Gloria, below) who bring positive problem-solving ability to social dilemmas. For all who dedicate themselves to the noble profession of early childhood education, such examples abound. These experiences provide the grist that keeps many early childhood professionals in the field.

The favorite dessert of thirty-nine-month-old Jackson is peaches in syrup. On this day, Jackson is sitting at the end of the table and dramatically extolling his favorite dessert—both verbally and with arm gestures. With his right arm, Jackson accidentally sweeps his bowl of peaches to the floor! He puts his head on the table and begins to yowl! Teacher Amy gets up from her seat and arrives quickly, calming Jackson and telling him it was an accident and that as soon as they clean this one up, Jackson can have another serving.

On the floor with Jackson, Amy realizes what fifty-six-month-old seatmate Gloria already knows: There are no more peaches! Amy slows down the cleaning process while trying to think of what to do. Finally, she has no alternative but to get Jackson back on his chair. There in front of Jackson is a bowl of peaches! Amy and Jackson look at Gloria and the empty space before her on the table. Gloria explains, "Jackson was crying loud. He needed them more than me." Amy asks Gloria if she is sure she wants to give Jackson her dessert. She nods yes. The two thank Gloria profusely. Amy has an appreciative talk with Gloria later in the day.

Amy, a child care professional in Minnesota, told me this story a few years ago. When I shared it once at a conference, a participant objected that the teacher should not have let Gloria give up her peaches. She stated that Jackson had to learn the natural consequence of spilling his dessert. I thanked her for her comment and gently suggested another view. Teacher Amy did the right thing by asking Gloria if she really wanted to take this action. By choosing to do so, the child was learning about showing compassion. Gloria would have gotten an entirely different message if the teacher had forbidden her generous gesture.

For thirty-nine-month-old Jackson, the philosophical message from being given the peaches might well have been that there are caring people in the world and that caring for each other in a time of need is a good thing. (Amy quietly explained this to Jackson.) Amy told me she never forgot Gloria's act of kindness. It seems like important life lessons happened here for all concerned.

In terms of the democratic life skills, Jackson was still working on DLS 2, expressing strong emotions in nonhurting ways, instead of putting his head on the table and yowling. (Heck, last week I did the same thing when I spilled my last glass of . . . prune juice!) Gloria was showing skills 3, 4, and 5: solving a problem creatively and cooperatively, accepting unique human qualities in others, and acting intelligently and ethically. The preschooler demonstrated a selfless use of conflict management (perhaps preventing an outburst of historic proportion in doing so) and of social problem solving. Young children can and do show impressive conflict-management skills—after consistent adult modeling and teaching.

The Curriculum of Conflict Management

As famed vintage books *The Giving Tree* and *The Rainbow Fish* illustrate, the matter of the happiness of one vis-à-vis the happiness of the group is an important issue to raise and discuss even with preschool children. Leading these practical yet philosophical discussions is a valid use of group meetings. Professor Thomas Wartenberg, author of *Big Ideas for Little Kids: Teaching Philosophy through Children's Literature*, believes such discussions should happen as a regular part of even the early childhood daily program. Besides, because such discussions often involve high-quality picture books (like those mentioned here) and shared self-expression, most young children readily engage in these ethics-building activities (Goodnough 2010).

Building on Wartenberg's approach, for those familiar with *The Rainbow Fish* by Marcus Pfister: Should the rainbow fish give away his scales to have friends? How about his last scale? And should you give a mouse a cookie, or a moose a muffin? And is it all right for the grouchy ladybug to be grouchy? What do you think about how the ladybug showed she was feeling grouchy? Such questions posed to children during open-ended group meetings make for brain-building bottoms-on-carpet-squares philosophical discussions.

In leading philosophical group meetings, even with preschoolers, teachers act as friendly facilitators, encouraging discussion and thought. Adults should resist the temptation to deliver moral mini lectures on the meaning of the experience as they see it. Kids in encouraging settings think good things on their own, and they develop their own good thinking in the process.

So the curriculum of conflict management comes down to both prepared and spontaneous lessons, often in the form of group meetings, that fulfill any of Glasser's three types of meetings: open-ended, educational, and problem-solving. To help to make the topics more real, a teacher can use books, puppet plays, and issue discussions, as well as follow-up activities such as story pictures in the art area and featured books in a library corner.

Early childhood professionals can design curricula that address the specific needs of the children in the group. Some resources on the topic, put out by NAEYC, aid budding emotional-social educational programs. The resources can be found on the NAEYC web pages related to ethically teaching and teaching for ethics learning (https://store.naeyc.org/product-subject/165). Commercial programs like Second Step and Responsive Classroom also provide curriculum guides for teaching about conflict management.

In summary, early childhood professionals in encouraging learning communities take an integrated approach to teaching conflict-management skills to young children, using these practices:

- Through group meetings, they make discussions of ethics-building, philosophical issues part of the curriculum. In these meetings, adults establish guidelines with the group, which they can then use as talking points in conflict mediations.

- At the same time, during disputes, teachers model and teach the skills of conflict mediation, nudging children toward resolving their own conflicts through negotiation.

Certainly, society needs more citizens who can engage civilly and competently in social problem solving, conflict management, and mediation with others! The early childhood profession continues to lead the way through modeling what even young children can accomplish by way of social problem solving. The noble work of teaching these abilities begins in the minds of early childhood professionals who model and teach these abilities every day.

The Five-Finger Formula for Conflict Mediation

The *five-finger formula for conflict mediation* (first discussed on pages 39–40) is a technique for use in conflict mediation. In researching formulas that early childhood professionals might use for mediating conflicts, I discovered a variety of formulas ranging from three steps to ten steps and more (really!). The three-stepper is to identify the problem, decide on a solution, and implement the solution. All other formulas build off these three steps, including the five-finger formula.

One emphasis in the five-finger formula is to make sure everyone has calmed down before starting—thumbkin, the first step. The formula also emphasizes true mediation in the sense that the adult works hard to get agreement from the children during the deliberation steps, 2, 3, and 4—pointer, tall guy, and ringer. (When mediating with emerging language and English-language learners, the leader provides spoken prompts and then reads the child's nonverbal cues to determine agreement.) In all cases, the teacher follows up during the implementation of the solution with monitoring, congratulations, guidance talks, and facilitating reconciliation—the fifth step, pinky.

The five steps are as follows:

Thumbkin: Cool everyone down, starting with yourself. (Use cool-down time and/or moving from the scene as needed—see chapter 6.)

Pointer: Get each child to agree on how each viewed the problem. (Do not interpret who was right and wrong; just move each child to agreement about how each saw the issue.)

Tall guy: Brainstorm possible solutions. (Use wait time to encourage ideas from the children. If they are unwilling or unable to express ideas, suggest possibilities and work for agreement from each child on a solution that is fair to each child. Your ability here to read nonverbal language is important.)

Ringer: Facilitate the implementation of the idea that the children have agreed on. (Do so even if the solution is not what you had in mind—this is their solution more than yours. Just make sure it is relatively fair and agreeable to each child).

Pinky: Monitor and positively acknowledge the successful mediation and solution. (If needed, use the teachable moment afforded by the successful mediation to hold a guidance talk with one or more of the children. The GT is for teaching what they can do next time instead.) Nudge children toward reconciliation if it did not come out of the mediation itself.

To help remember the steps, you might write the five on a card, post them on the wall, or just count them off on your fingers.

When and How to Use Five-Finger Mediation

Not all situations require conflict mediation. Waiting to see if children can resolve an issue themselves is often a sensible approach. From experience, the adult will know when to intervene, particularly in order to prevent imminent harm and serious disruption. Calm first, then mediate.

When intervening, the five-finger formula can be a guide for conflict management with

- individual children through guidance talks;

- groups of two or three through conflict mediation; and/or

- the full group through group meetings.

Early childhood professionals tend to follow the five steps most closely in mediation situations and more informally in guidance talks and group meetings. In the full group setting, step one, calming everyone down, usually is not necessary. In both group meetings and guidance talks, steps three and four often blend together. This is fine.

In any of the three situations, the mediator does not need a master's degree to make conflict mediation work. The technique does not require textbook perfection—as long as the teacher leads as mediator-in-chief (and not judge and jury), good enough is almost always good enough. During mediation, the teacher is fair and firm but friendly in making sure the children take turns speaking and listening and working through the process.

In five-finger mediation, the adult remains fair to both children, even if one seems a bit more the perpetrator and the other a bit more the victim. The equalized give-and-take in mediation tends to be nonpunitively humbling for the child who forced the conflict and gratifying for the child who might have been victimized. The object of the mediator is to restore equilibrium through teaching both children the art of give-and-take, so restoring each child to a person in good standing in the group.

Again, when mediation is done well enough, each child sustains his or her status as fully accepted, worthwhile members of the group. This outcome reduces the likelihood of a bully-victim cycle that can be reinforced in traditional punish-the-perp, comfort-the-victim discipline. Traditional discipline tends to leave the conflict unresolved. The punished child often feels continued anger toward the comforted child, who has been put in a diminished and vulnerable position through obvious dependence on the intervening adult.

If, after mediation, a child still seems upset or needs more coaching about a mistaken behavior, the adult follows up with a guidance talk. Give children time to reconcile if they need it, but do actively support the effort. Mediators should smile if later or the next day the same two children who previously fought are doing an activity together. (I bet the reader has seen this happen—if not, you will.)

High-Level Mediation

Teachers use the five-finger formula with a high degree of leadership that involves direct coaching in the following situations:

- Children are just learning the mediation process.

- Children are either just beginning to use spoken language or speak a language different from the teacher's.

- Children have difficulty managing emotions in conflict situations.

In these situations, actively coach children to use words to express their feelings and perceptions. Offer words on behalf of the child, but always check the child's nonverbal reactions for agreement. In all uses of the five-finger formula, the early childhood professional works hard to maintain a balance between advocacy for the less-powerful party and mediation fairness toward both parties. Being firm, friendly, and balanced is key.

 Thirty-two-month-old Brandi has been pushing her bus along the floor. She pushes it so hard it goes clear to the other side of the room. Ronald, another thirty-two-month old, picks it up and runs away with it. Brandi screams and runs after him, grabbing at his shirt. Ronald trips and falls. Holding the bus, he yells from the floor, "My bus!" "My bus!" retorts Brandi and stands over Ronald with clenched fists. (Big property dispute here.)

Teacher Arnetta arrives. She sits down next to Ronald and helps Brandi sit by her other side.

Step One: Calming

"You both are upset," Arnetta says. "Let's take three deep breaths and wait a minute to cool off. Then we can solve this problem." She gently takes the bus from Ronald and says, "I will hold the bus, Ronald, until we take care of this problem."

Arnetta and the children each take three deep breaths. She then asks them to sit still while she times out a minute on her watch. Arnetta asks both children if they are calm. They seem calm enough to continue.

Step Two: Agreeing about the Problem

ARNETTA: Ronald, I need to hear from Brandi what happened. Then I need to hear from you. Let's listen to Brandi.

BRANDI: My bus. Ronald took it. (*Ronald has his teeth clenched. Arnetta puts a friendly hand on Ronald's shoulder.*)

ARNETTA: Were you rolling the bus on the floor and it rolled away?

BRANDI: Yes, and Ronald took it. He runned with it. (*Ronald is still gritting his teeth.*)

ARNETTA: Thank you, Brandi. Now let's hear from Ronald.

RONALD: It is my bus.

ARNETTA: The bus rolled to you, and you thought it was your turn to have it.

RONALD: (*Pause. The other two wait. He nods.*) My bus.

ARNETTA: You each thought the bus was yours. Is that the problem?

(*Both children nod.*)

Step Three: Brainstorming Possible Solutions

ARNETTA: What can we do to solve this problem? (*She pauses. Neither child comments.*) Oh look, Wyatt is done with the red truck! Can you give it to me, Wyatt? (*He does.*) How about if, Brandi, you get this one, and you roll your truck first. Then, Ronald, you roll your bus and see if it can catch Brandi's truck?

Step Four: Agreeing and Putting into Effect

Arnetta looks at each child. Brandi does not look thrilled.

BRANDI: Bus is my bus.

ARNETTA: Okay, Ronald, how about if you use the red truck? But you say if you want to push yours first or second. And you can roll it slow or fast.

RONALD: (*Tired of the process and wanting to play.*) Red truck. First! Brandi not gonna catch me. (*Ronald takes the red truck from Arnetta, gives it a push, and runs after it.*)

ARNETTA (*looking at Brandi*): Okay?

BRANDI (*looking at her teacher seriously*): Okay. (*Rolls her bus after Ronald, but slowly so she can retrieve it.*)

Step Five: Follow-Up

Arnetta watches the two play together with the bus and truck. She notices that Brandi retrieves Ronald's truck once and hands it to him. Ronald smiles and nods. Arnetta does too. Arnetta does nothing more. When two children who have been arguing end up playing together, the teacher knows that the mediation has gone successfully.

When emotions are high, teachers need to ensure that the calming process always happens. The provider does not abandon children when they are very upset—just postpones the mediation until the children are calm enough to talk and listen. Brandi and Ronald are both toddlers with emerging language, and Arnetta had to actively coach them to keep them in the process. She did, and the three came up with a solution that in the end the children accepted and put into action. Early childhood professionals use relationships they have built with children outside of conflicts to empower the mediation—and they're teaching street smarts!

Teachers insist on mediation not with every conflict but when there is a danger of serious harm or disruption. In the encouraging learning community, a consequence of children having a serious dispute *is* conflict mediation. After cooling down, if one or both children insist that they do not want to participate, use quiet toughness with the children and do not let them off easily. Make it known that if they opt out of the mediation, this means they have no say in the outcome.

Respect this out-choice when it is taken, but have guidance talks with the children later to discuss what happened. Make sure the children understand that conflict mediation is part of being a member of the community. "That is how we learn to solve problems with each other."

On occasion, you cannot fully mediate at the time of the conflict. That is understandable. But always take time to calm children down so there is no further harm or disruption. You may then tell the children you will discuss the problem later. Be flexible with what the passage of time may do for the children's perceptions. With time you may decide that a guidance talk with one or both children is more appropriate. Being a professional, you routinely make such judgments. Something should happen after the conflict, though, because you said it would. Teachers, like everyone, are only as good as their word.

Low-Level Mediation

The teacher works to move children from high-level mediation to low-level mediation. Older preschoolers who speak the same language as the teacher and have made progress with DLS 1 and 2 have the easiest time making the transition. Often the teacher may deal with one child still in need of high-level mediation and one ready for low-level. This is just one of the adjustments the early childhood professional routinely makes.

The key difference between high-level and low-level mediation is in the role of the teacher. In high-level, the teacher is working with children relatively new to mediation. These children may be showing survival behavior during the mediation as well as in the conflict. This is why firm but friendly leadership and active coaching are all a part of high-level mediation.

In low-level mediation, the teacher nudges children into assuming a greater role in the mediation. The professional sets the scene and offers cues, expecting (or at least hoping) that the children will take the lead in the resolution themselves. Still, the teacher remains ready to step in with active coaching if the children hit a roadblock.

Almost-fives Marci and Annette are working with small wooden tracks and trains. Carmen, fifty-two months old, asks to join them. The girls say no. Carmen offers to use blocks to build a station next to the tracks. "No way," the girls reply. Carmen says she will make a station "way over there and you can build the tracks to it." Marci says, "We're not playing with you." Annette says, "No way." In frustration, Carmen grabs two nearby Lincoln logs and bangs them hard against a box.

Provider Delphine arrives. She and Carmen sit away from the girls but within sight. Delphine helps Carmen calm down, and they talk quietly about what happened. After a minute or two, Carmen and the teacher approach Marci and Annette.

DELPHINE: Girls, I think we have a problem working together with the trains and blocks. Carmen is going to tell you how she sees the problem. Then I will ask you to say how you see the problem.

CARMEN: I just wanted to help you, and you wouldn't let me.

MARCI: But we were playing here just by ourselves.

ANNETTE: Yeah.

DELPHINE: (*Pauses*) Do you all see what the problem is? We have a guideline in our group that says, "We play together." How can we solve this problem so you three can play together?

MARCI: (*Pauses*) Carmen can build the station over there. We will build a track to it.

ANNETTE: But she's not playing with us, right?

MARCI: (*To Annette*) It would be better if we let her play. Trains and cars could come to the station. You could help me build the tracks to it.

ANNETTE: (*Deferring to Marci's leadership*) Okay. I'll get the tracks. You can play; build over there, Carmen.

Carmen grins, transports some blocks in a shopping cart to a spot four feet away, and starts building the station.

DELPHINE: Carmen, Marci, and Annette, you had a problem, and you solved it just about by yourselves. You remembered our guideline "We play together," and now you will have a station for trains and cars and a nice long track!

The three girls are already busy laying tracks and building the station. The three play together for the rest of work time.

A factor that adds greatly to children's progress with conflict-management skills lies in the developmentally appropriate learning environment. There is so much to do that is intriguing for young children that they want to do it, not argue. Notice that both the high-level and low-level mediations illustrated here had to do with conflicts that kept children from playing. You need a bus or truck to roll on the floor (property dispute) and you need to be able to share materials and space in order to play together (territory and privilege dispute). The bottom line is that unless the focus of activity is intriguing to young children, conflict-management skills won't matter much, and mediation won't be seen as worth the effort.

Especially at the beginning of the program year, children who show level three survival mistaken behavior have not yet gained a sense of belonging in the setting. A positive, trust-based relationship with an adult needs to be there for the child. Only then can the child manage stress well enough to see what the environment has to offer and become engaged. In the immediacy of a conflict, the adult-child relationship helps to carry the child through the conflicts that arise. Notice the calming that Delphine did with Carmen through a guidance talk before she and Carmen approached the two girls. With Delphine's quiet support, Carmen expressed her frustration with enough words to prompt the mediation.

In early childhood social situations, there are usually leaders and followers. In this vignette, Marci showed leadership, redressing an experimentation-level mistaken behavior. Marci needed teacher Delphine's cues to do so, but the child stepped up. Delphine, in my view, used guidance expertly here, focusing more on how to solve the problem (this time and hopefully next time) than on the wrong Marci and Annette committed by not initially letting Carmen play. We consider this illustration to be low-level mediation because after Carmen shared her frustration, Marci, with Delphine's cues, took the lead in resolving the conflict. So that they could keep playing, Marci went along.

Notice, too, how Delphine followed up by positively acknowledging the achievement of the three girls by working through the dispute. No bells were rung or group-wide attention drawn, but Delphine sustained the encouraging learning community for these three by her low-level mediation—and for any bystanders who likely watched the events.

Peer Negotiation

Children need to have basic needs met, including a firm sense of belonging, in order to be able to negotiate disputes on their own. Otherwise, stress levels, which likely contributed to the conflict in the first place, will lead to survival behaviors that undermine the trust and back-and-forth communication that are needed. This means that each child basically needs to have gained DLS 1 (belonging and self-worth) and DLS 2 (expressing emotions in nonhurting ways). Typically, for negotiation to happen, at least one child also needs to be in the process of gaining DLS 3, 4, and 5. Often this child assumes a leadership role and scaffolds the negotiation. (In the illustration below, the child who does this is Nakisha.) If both preschoolers in an encouraging learning setting are working on the three growth life skills, negotiations often occur on a cooperative basis.

For children to learn to negotiate, practice at mediation with adults is invaluable. Experience with solving problems peaceably has two blended benefits. First, it tells children that managing conflicts with civil words is feasible and expected in the learning setting—so it is no big deal for them to try. Second, participating in mediation teaches the skills that young children need to negotiate.

These skills center around perspective taking, understanding how the other sees the issue, and *self-reporting*—that is, the honest communication of one child about how he or she feels about the issue in ways that don't make the other child more upset. Preschoolers use these skills intuitively rather than analytically, but what is important is that they can and do use them.

The following illustration of peer negotiation is such a classic, I had to borrow it (and the follow-up discussion) from my textbook (Gartrell 2014).

Nakisha and Suel Lin were caring for a variety of dolls in the kindergarten housekeeping area. They both reached for the last doll that had to be fed, bathed, and put to bed. They started quarreling that each had it first, and Suel Lin took Nakisha's arm and started squeezing it.

"Stop, that hurts," exclaimed Nakisha. "Use your words!"

"I can't find any," yelled Suel Lin.

"Then get Power Sock," Nakisha demanded. Both girls, still holding part of the doll, walked over and got Power Sock. "I will wear him, Suel Lin, and you tell Sock."

Suel Lin said to Sock, "Baby needs a bath. We both want to do it."

"Both do it," said Sock.

The two girls put back Power Sock and returned to the housekeeping area, still both holding the doll! One girl washed the top half, the other the bottom half. Then Suel Lin held the doll and fed it while Nakisha read a story to the other dolls already in bed. Suel Lin said, "Here's baby; do you want to read another story?"

"Yeah," said Nakisha, who read another story while Suel Lin rubbed the babies' backs as they lay in their beds.

(In her journal entry documenting these events, the student teacher reflected, "I couldn't believe how Nakisha and Suel Lin solved the problem! I didn't have to do anything!")

Defining the problem: Nakisha acknowledged her feelings calmly enough that Suel Lin let go and agreed to negotiate with her by using the Power Sock. Suel Lin forgot a guideline when she was squeezing Nakisha's arm. Conventional discipline would call for a punishment such as a scolding or sitting on a time-out chair. This result probably would have made Suel Lin feel angry and ashamed and Nakisha feel victimized. The student teacher refrained from intervening long enough to see if Nakisha could handle the situation. By doing so, she opened the door for negotiation and created an opportunity for the children to find a mutually satisfactory solution.

Reaching a solution: Nakisha and Suel Lin used a sock puppet prop usually used by the teachers to mediate a solution. Nakisha was more experienced with Power Sock than Suel Lin and took the initiative to request Sock to help them negotiate. The discussion did not involve a lot of verbal articulation. Nonetheless, their negotiation was creative and peaceable and would have made most teachers smile. The self-esteem of each child was sustained enough that they were able to finish the task together.

Very often in successful peer negotiation, one child (usually the older) is able to manage her emotions and control the impulse to hurt back. In working to solve the problem in the midst of a stressful situation, Nakisha showed this emotional-social competence.

Bringing successful closure: The two children continued to play together and did so with a high degree of cooperation. In contrast to conventional discipline, mediation and peer negotiation reduce residual resentment and continued conflicts into the future.

The ability of children to negotiate conflicts indicates that important goals of an encouraging community are being attained. The children are gaining in perspective taking and emotional-social competence and are progressing through the democratic life skills. They are beginning to learn lifelong language and communications skills. They are also learning important lessons about friendship.

Peace Props

Especially with young children, peace props can help the conflict-management process. Teachers can use peace props at either high-level or low-level mediation. In addition, as Nakisha and Suel Lin showed here, peace props can help children make the transition from mediation to peer negotiation. Because young children are concrete in their thinking, peace props help to make social problem solving real. Here are some ideas for peace props:

Peace (or Power) socks: Peace socks are sock puppets that adults teach children to use. (Puppets of all kinds tend to be magical to young children.) In mediation, the teacher wears the sock at the beginning to effect step one and set up step two. The teacher decides whether to continue wearing the sock or to pass it to each child as the mediation proceeds. In peer negotiation, the children have learned how to use the peace sock and may or may not exchange it between them as they talk, listen, and resolve the dispute. (Nakisha kept the sock and demonstrated that in this instance, it was indeed a power sock.)

Talking sticks: These are decorated ceremonial sticks that work in the same way as peace socks. They are held horizontally, parallel to the chest, with the individual holding each end. The adult or child says his or her piece, then passes the stick to the other. A variation on the talking stick is the talking rock. Obviously, with hard objects children need to learn how to use them—often the subject of group meetings. (These peace props also remind the adult to make sure the children are calm before beginning the mediation!)

Gigi Holt, a Head Start teacher in northern Minnesota, taught the use of the talking stick to her class. Each child in the group made a talking stick and uniquely decorated it with natural materials and glue. On Friday of that week, the children took their talking sticks home. On Monday a curious parent called Gigi and asked about the stick. It seems that Mom and Dad were having an argument. Their Head Start child got the stick and had them use it to settle the matter!

Talk and listen chairs: One chair is marked as the talking chair; another one or two are marked as listening chairs. When children are having a dispute, they and a teacher move to the chairs and take turns switching between the chairs until the matter is resolved. A teacher once told me that she knew the chairs were working when, in December, two children were quarreling. One said, "Let's go to them chairs." The other said, "Yeah!" They went to the chairs, spoke and listened, and took care of the problem on their own.

Concluding Thoughts
(Warning: Mild Author Rant)

It's a shame that more K–12 schools do not make social problem solving central to the curriculum, through direct teaching and using conflict mediation. How much bullying and violence (both during the school years and after) could be prevented by this shift in philosophical perspective in our education system? Of course, such change will happen only to the extent that curricula, methods, and assessments can be more developmentally appropriate at the K–12 level—as has long been the case in quality early childhood care and education programs.

Seeing peer negotiation work makes teachers of all age levels smile, but especially teachers of young children. The language facility, problem-solving competence, and civil attitudes that children demonstrate when they manage a conflict peaceably lie at the heart of what being a truly successful student is. Even more, these abilities, at the core of the five democratic life skills, are what can ensure the continuation of our society into the twenty-second century.

Discussion Questions

An element of being an early childhood professional is respecting the children, parents, and educators with whom you are working by keeping identities private. In completing follow-up activities, please respect the privacy of all concerned.

1. Share an account of a high- or a low-level mediation or a peer negotiation that you observed or interviewed a teacher about. Give some reasons for which of the three you think it was. Share a self-report assessment of what you learned about conflict management in early childhood from this experience.

2. Discuss benefits to young children of learning conflict management skills as they move on in their education. Include both academic and social benefits.

3. Do you see value in having philosophical and ethical group discussions with young children, such as after reading select picture books with them?

   a. If you do, what do you think the role of the teacher should be in leading the discussions?

   b. If you don't, please share your thinking about this position.

4. Ideally, social problem solving will be at the core of the education children receive after preschool. But if children's K–12 schooling is more traditionally academic, discuss the value of teaching conflict management in early childhood.

Key Concepts

Definitions of the Key Concepts can be found in the glossary on pages 177–84.

Conflict management   Low-level mediation

Conflict mediation   Peer negotiation

High-level mediation   Self-report

CHAPTER 9

Comprehensive Guidance: The Practice of Liberation Teaching

COMPREHENSIVE GUIDANCE MEANS PURPOSEFULLY INTEGRATING separate guidance methods in order to provide caring leadership to young children who experience serious conflicts. The conflicts these children cause and fall into are level three survival mistaken behaviors. Due to challenging environmental and/or physiological factors, the children are reacting to amygdala-driven toxic stress. They become oversensitive to threats in their environments. When they perceive a threat—sometimes in everyday situations not threatening to others—they react with the survival behaviors of fighting, freezing, and/or fleeing.

In terms of the equilibrium of the encouraging community, the most challenging survival behavior is the fight reaction, which expresses itself in reactive and instrumental aggression. As a mistaken effort to deal with their stress, some children impulsively lash out when they feel threatened. Others develop mistaken proactive strategies that involve survival behaviors to intentionally fend off perceived threats. These kids intentionally cause level three conflicts, feeling that the best defense is a strong offense. Too often adults respond to aggressive behavior in punitive ways that further aggravate the child's stress. Rejection and resulting mistrust of others make relationships all the more difficult for these children. They internalize negative self-messages and can develop long-term difficulties with learning, behavior, and social relations—the stress-rejection cycle.

Buffering from the Start

Buffering happens through intentional liberation teaching. Children who come into our programs with toxic stress need immediate and long-term proactive support. The teacher does not give up on these children. Instead, early childhood professionals work together to observe, form relationships with, and guide these children to feel safe, worthy, and capable of learning. Buffering means structuring the environment and relationships to help the child gain the two basic democratic life skills.

A challenge for teachers is that survival behavior often includes difficulty in trusting and forming relationships with others. The buffering process hinges on the adult simply being stronger than the child—being unrelentingly positive. The adult uses acknowledgment, contact talks, friendly physical proximity, and reciprocal relationships with family members to win the child over. Then the long-term process of helping the child build resilience can begin.

Resiliency is the combination of the child's emotional ability to manage stress and the social ability to interact positively and purposefully in interactive experiences. The hallmark of success in helping children find resiliency is their ability to manage stress and respond in nonhurting ways during conflicts. Resiliency means the child has largely achieved DLS 1 and 2 and is working on DLS 3, 4, and 5.

Comprehensive Guidance: A Seven-Step Approach

Even with a teacher's best efforts at buffering from day one, the problems some children face force them into survival behavior patterns that make comprehensive guidance necessary. Comprehensive guidance typically has seven steps that guide early childhood professionals when dealing with children who exhibit extreme and continuing survival behaviors. The steps can be followed formally or informally, and not all seven may be necessary, depending on the situation. Before choosing to use comprehensive guidance, teachers first need to recognize that a child's mistaken behaviors are happening with such regularity and intensity that a coordinated approach is necessary. Collaboration, adults working together, then becomes key. Usually a lead teacher serves as the captain in the process, working with others on a single team. Here are the seven steps:

1. **Observe and record patterns of mistaken behavior.** A pattern of atypical, extreme, or inappropriate behavior for more than a few days indicates

serious unmet physical or emotional needs. The teacher observes if there are certain days, times of the day, or activities that tend to set the child off. Important: The teacher keeps a log of the patterns observed.

2. **Build the relationships.** A child facing life challenges needs a helping relationship with a teacher who acknowledges the child's efforts, achievements, anxieties, and frustrations. Building a relationship with the family from the time the child enters the program is also essential.

3. **Use consistent guidance intervention techniques.** The teacher uses buffering practices during days or times that the child is particularly vulnerable for level three mistaken behavior. These might include modifications of the program and having an adult shadow the child. The early childhood professional responds in firm but friendly ways to the mistaken behavior, using intervention practices such as calming techniques, guidance talks, and conflict mediation.

4. **Obtain additional information.** The teacher seeks to understand the child and the child's behavior more fully by studying charted incidents and talking with the child, staff, and family.

5. **Hold IGP meeting.** If the frequency and severity of conflicts are not noticeably reduced after using steps one through four, the staff holds an Individual Guidance Plan (IGP) meeting with the family, teaching staff, and other relevant adults. The team uses the problem-solving process outlined in the Individual Guidance Plan (see IGP form on page 185 in appendix).

6. **Implement guidance plan.** The team works together to put the IGP into operation. The staff continues to build relationships with the child and family and adapts the educational program to increase opportunities for the child to succeed, thereby reducing the child's propensity for conflict. Referrals for assessments by special education or other helping professionals may be a part of the plan. Families need to be accepting of assessments used, which is why meeting with the family is vital.

7. **Monitor guidance plan.** The staff reviews the plan, communicates with families, and modifies the plan as needed. If necessary, the staff holds a second IGP meeting.

Comprehensive Guidance
in a Case of Reactive Aggression

Eduardo, aged fifty-eight months, came to the preschool program partway through the year. In a previous town, Eduardo had witnessed alcohol-induced violence in his family, beginning from when he was an infant. Mother Jen and Eduardo had fled to a shelter to escape domestic abuse. With the assistance of others, he and his mom had relocated to this community and gotten into the support network of an economic assistance agency. Eduardo was known to show withdrawn behavior with sudden bouts of reactive aggression. He was thought to be a victim of *childhood post-traumatic stress syndrome*, and he had difficulty responding to new situations and new people.

Teacher Cora let Eduardo observe without participating when he started at the preschool, and she spent quiet moments with the child whenever she could. One girl in the group, Penny, showed empathy beyond her age. Cora asked Penny to quietly help Eduardo to join in activities, but only if Eduardo wanted to. Penny was up to the task. On more than one occasion, Cora observed the two children doing things together. Eduardo wasn't saying much to anyone yet, but Cora thought he would in time.

Penny was popular in the group, and another child or two began to join Penny and Eduardo while they were doing things. Cora was pleased when Eduardo played with Jerome and Sandy in the dramatic play area. She worried about putting too much responsibility on Penny, though this one-in-a-thousand kid didn't seem to mind.

At the art center, Eduardo really seemed to like the color red. One day the main color available at the table was red: crayons, markers, paint, and even red-dyed macaroni and red glue. Another day there was only red playdough. Eduardo did not need Penny's help to engage in these activities. Though he was still not joining the group for music activities, after about two weeks, Cora noticed Eduardo quietly singing one of the songs to himself as he was looking at a book—naturally *Red: A Crayon's Story.* Cora figured it would only be a matter of time before Eduardo joined the large group.

Almost daily at one point or another, Eduardo would dramatically lose emotional control. On occasion, Cora needed to use the passive bear hug with the child, but she made a point of doing things with Eduardo after he calmed down. (The passive bear hugs were hard on Cora; Eduardo was a big kid for his age.) Cora sensed that Eduardo was not resenting her because of the interventions, and gradually the meltdowns happened less frequently. Eduardo's mom said that he was reluctant about going to school for the first week. With phone support from Cora with Jen, Eduardo made it each day. During the second week, getting Eduardo to the program became easier. From Mom's standpoint, like Cora's, the child was beginning to settle in.

Below are how Eduardo's teacher Cora used each of the seven steps.

1. Observe and record pattern of mistaken behavior

Observation is the basic tool teachers use to learn about children and their behavior. Adults especially observe times of the day or time blocks during the schedule when the child is apt to experience conflicts. Many strategies for observation are out there. I favor a relatively simple anecdotal observation tool, which can be adapted either for an electronic device or used in the ancient form of a hard copy:

Date and time:

Child's name:

Observer's name:

Observation:
(Objective and specific: Just what is said and done; no personal interpretations)

Inferences:
(Adult's balanced and thoughtful interpretations of and reflections about the recorded observations)

Cora, along with assistant teacher Venetia, and work-study student Jinada could not miss Eduardo's outbursts. The three set about trying to observe what triggered them. Their approach was to have Venetia or Jinada do anecdotal observations during the time blocks that seemed most difficult for Eduardo: just before breakfast, late in the morning during work time, and midafternoon during a second work time. Both Venetia and Jinada used the same process: date and time; child's name; observer's name; objective recording of what was said and done; and reflection about the meaning of the events observed. The write-ups typically did not go longer than a page or two. These completed forms provided documentation at staff and Individual Guidance Plan meetings and were an important component of the comprehensive guidance.

The staff concluded that some days were harder than others. Eduardo seemed more tired on days that did not go well. On these days, Eduardo began having conflicts right away in the morning. With the exception of Penny, Eduardo acted out against children, particularly when he thought they were encroaching on his territory or were about to claim things he was using or intending to use. When Cora or Venetia arrived quickly, they could sometimes head off a blow up.

2. Build the relationships

Cora, Venetia, and Jinada each had daily contact talks with Eduardo. Eduardo seemed drawn to Venetia, so Venetia spent quality time with him when he first arrived. The team found that easing Eduardo into the program upon his arrival was an investment of time that kept tantrums to a minimum for at least the first half of the day. This practice meant that Cora worked with Jinada each morning to greet other children and get breakfast ready to serve. It kept them busy, but Cora and the program's director, Anna, thought the change in routine was an investment in the day worth making.

As lead teacher, Cora also worked on relationship building with mother Jen. Every time they met, Cora made sure to use compliment sandwiches in discussing Eduardo. Cora made herself available for Jen to contact mornings before school and any time after school until nine o'clock in the evening. She debated whether to do this but decided to give Jen her cell phone number so Jen could reach her in time of need. Jen appreciated Cora's efforts, saying no one had taken an interest in her son like this before.

A month into the program, Eduardo's dramatic conflicts diminished to every other day or so—fewer, but still too many. Less-dramatic conflicts that nonetheless required adult intervention were still happening daily. The boy's relations with all three staff members were getting steadier.

3. Use consistent guidance intervention techniques

The staff used guidance talks and conflict mediation just about every day with Eduardo. Helping him get calm first was a necessity. The staff sometimes delayed further intervention steps until Eduardo got over whatever he was upset about. By way of prevention, Jinada often shadowed Eduardo at peak conflict times and sat by the child in groups and during meals. This level of monitoring was necessary because Eduardo was capable of doing real harm. The staff routinely used quadruple compliment sandwiches in guidance talks with the boy.

With these efforts, Eduardo was lashing out less and interacting with others more. He still lost emotional control frequently during conflicts, and he was still having conflicts each day that needed staff attention.

4. Obtain additional information

For legal reasons, developmental records concerning Eduardo were not available to the staff. Because of the nature of the rescue and relocation, any previous professionals who might have worked with Jen and Eduardo were unavailable. Getting such permission from parents and meeting with all who have prior professional experience with the family is important, though this can be challenging to acquire.

5. Hold IGP meeting

Cora held an Individual Guidance Plan meeting with Venetia, Jinada, Director Anna, and Jen. They had to reschedule twice due to Jen's unpredictable work schedule. At the meeting, they agreed to take the comprehensive guidance to a formal level through discussing and completing an IGP form and following the steps in comprehensive guidance more formally. Jen agreed to have Eduardo go through an assessment for emotional stress and possible admission to the Early Childhood Special Education (ECSE) program offered through the school district. Together they planned a coordinated approach to take with Eduardo, at home and in the program.

The plan called for an early childhood special education screening, a physical for Eduardo at the neighborhood free health clinic, a minimum of five contact talks with Eduardo each day in the program, and a minimum of three contact talks between Jen and Eduardo each day at home. One of the talks was to occur during a regular bedtime story Jen was starting with Eduardo.

The staff saw that Jen appreciated the meeting. She realized that all involved were taking extra steps on behalf of her son. Through her involvement, Jen had definitely reached engagement level two: accepting information and working together with early childhood professionals on behalf of the child. Jen was to meet with Cora every two weeks, and the two would discuss guidance techniques Jen could use with Eduardo as well as how the IGP was working. The team was to meet again in six weeks to review progress with the IGP.

6. Implement guidance plan

The staff and Jen implemented the plan as best they could. The staff continued to use contact talks and prevention measures, along with guidance talks and mediation when Eduardo acted out. The emphasis on calming Eduardo during conflicts became less necessary but was consciously continued. Jen reported to Cora that she and Eduardo were reading every night—Eduardo insisted on it! The other mother-son contact talks were less formally handled, but Jen said that Eduardo seemed to be listening to her more. The two were also making a trip each week to a place of interest. Jen started these mother-son dates on her own, and they both were enjoying them. One stop Eduardo loved was to a local fast-food restaurant, where the boy could expend energy using the elaborate climber there to his heart's content. With these steps, Jen had clearly progressed to family engagement level two, implementing an education program at home.

The screening was completed. On the basis of the screening, the ECSE teacher formally approved a follow-up in-depth assessment for Eduardo to determine program eligibility for early childhood special education. A date for the assessment was pending.

The staff was satisfied that the plan was being implemented. They set a date with Jen for the meeting to review the IGP. This time Jen made the meeting.

7. Monitor guidance plan

During the review meeting, the staff and Jen went over each item on the IGP. They all felt Eduardo was making progress. Both in the program and at home, the adults were feeling more gratified and less frustrated with Eduardo's behavior. They had observed fewer tantrums and an increase in positive interactions in both settings. This meeting happened two months into the program. The team agreed to meet again after the special education assessment and review developments at that time. Cora asked director Anna to follow up to get the early childhood special education assessment completed.

Conducting Successful IGP Meetings*

Several conditions must be in place for any Individual Guidance Plan to be successful. Starting when the child first enters the program, the staff works with parents to help them move toward level of engagement two, taking an interest in the education program for the child. Family members must at least be moving into level two to be able to participate successfully in the IGP. This being said, the formula for successful IGPs is always the same: the staff and parents agree on the problem, agree on what needs to be done about the problem, do it, and monitor the results. As mentioned, collaboration in taking the guidance-based problem-solving approach is key. The IGP process can be handled informally sometimes, without a face-to-face meeting. Other times there is no substitute for getting all parties together in the same room.

IGP meetings roughly follow the same steps as conflict mediation, the steps the teacher uses with children in the classroom.

With the leadership of the lead professional, the team discusses the meeting dynamics and possible outcomes, which the group together will decide. One staff member agrees to be recorder. It is agreed which staff members will attend. The staff discusses the importance of a compliment sandwich approach by which any staff member expressing a concern also gives at least two compliments about the child's/family's effort, progress, or attitude. The compliment sandwich strategy helps to keep the IGP positive and on track.

At the meeting, here are five steps to follow:

1. **The leader makes everyone as comfortable as possible** with greetings, positive comments, and a brief explanation of the meeting. The leader lets everyone know that this is a meeting where we all work together for a common goal: the good of the child. The leader emphasizes that agreement on decisions is important and introduces the recorder who writes down key points and decisions on a chart, which everyone can see. Staff members either establish or at least keep in mind guidelines for the meeting such as the following:

   - Everyone has a common purpose that will help to make the meeting positive: the good of the child.

   - Each member of the group receives respect from all others, even when views differ.

---

* The following is adapted from the *Instructor's Manual for A Guidance Approach for the Encouraging Classroom*, 5th ed. (2010). Thanks to Wadsworth/Cengage for permission to use this material.

- All members work to separate facts from interpretations of facts.

- Each member needs to be responsible for what he or she chooses to share.

- Each member remains open to new thoughts and ways of thinking.

- Decisions made at the meeting are by consensus.

2. **The leader assists everyone to agree on what the problem is.** The leader provides necessary documentation and interpretation and asks the others to contribute. She or he encourages participants to separate facts from interpretations in their presentations and models this practice throughout the meeting. The recorder writes down only what is agreed on.

3. **The group brainstorms all possible nonpunitive strategies they can think of.** With the recorder's assistance, the leader organizes the brainstorming around components such as some of these:

- in-class conflict prevention strategies

- in-class conflict interventions

- in-class relationship-building responses

- in-class long-term remediation strategies

- in-home conflict-response strategies

- in-home togetherness-building responses

- in-home long-term remediation strategies

- referral strategies for additional assessment and assistance

- realistic resources needed to implement the plan

4. **The group decides on a plan using the most promising strategies for any of the components addressed in step three.** This is where negotiation, flexibility, and compromise provide the key. If the group is in disagreement about any parts of the plan, its potential for success is endangered. The recorder seeks clarification of major points and gives a written summary of the strategies agreed on.

5. **The group decides the role of each member in using the plan and sets a second meeting date to monitor progress.** The leader and family decide on a staff member who will be team leader on the plan. This person will assist the family with implementing their part of the plan, including any

referral processes. The team leader will also ensure continuity among the staff in accomplishing the classroom goals of the plan. He or she will provide coordination between home and classroom in carrying out the plan. After setting a time and date for the follow-up meeting, the team leader works to ensure that all members can and do attend. The recorder gets a copy of the completed IGP to the plan leader and the family.

The second meeting to review and possibly modify the IGP is often conducted more informally than the main meeting. Follow-up contact after the second meeting is less formal still. A final or exit IGP meeting is sometimes held to celebrate success or to decide what additional actions may be necessary. Follow-up of some kind is important. The IGP meeting is not the end in itself, but a means to a better end for the child, the family, and the entire encouraging learning community.

Comprehensive Guidance in a Case of Instrumental Aggression[*]

A second illustration of comprehensive guidance at work is the following vignette involving instrumental aggression. Note the collaboration among the teaching team members, including the director, and with the mother. Robin Bakken, a skilled and experienced teacher at the Campus Child Care Center of Bemidji State University in Minnesota, is the lead professional in this study. (In an indication of the state of early childhood care and education in the society, due to a lack of funding, the campus-based laboratory program at Bemidji State closed the year after I retired.)

Mazie, aged forty-six months, started in Robin's child care room in the middle of the year. Mazie's parents told Robin that Mazie had been asked to leave her previous child care because of her behavior. In the previous program, Mazie had gone from being the youngest child in the group the first year to being the oldest child the following September. Her parents suggested that she was bullied by older children the first year and perhaps felt rejected the second year when the younger children received more attention from the provider. The parents thought that Mazie was causing frequent conflicts for these reasons.

Thanks to NAEYC's *Young Children* for permission to adapt this January 2008 Guidance Matters column for the book. Thanks also to Robin Bakken for her years of good leadership at Campus Childcare.

Mazie's sister, Emma, five years older, had attended Robin's center. Other teachers told Robin that Emma was a sweet child from a stable family. The parents decided to give Mazie a new start at a program with which her family was familiar. With more than thirty years' experience as a teacher, Robin felt her room would be a good fit for Mazie.

Mazie's behavior did not stand out to Robin during the Getting to Know You conference or during Mazie's first day in the group. But on the second day, when it was time to wash hands and come to breakfast, Mazie continued playing with toys. Robin approached the child knowing it was important to balance Mazie's need to get used to a new setting with the staff's need to establish routines. But a conflict followed, and Mazie turned over a child-sized couch, screamed loudly, and reacted dramatically for fifteen minutes to Robin's quiet attempts to calm her.

This wasn't the end of Mazie's displays of aggression. Every day, when her personal plans were disrupted, Mazie acted out against other children and teachers. She used a variety of aggressive techniques to get what she wanted. If someone had something of interest to Mazie, she just took it. Daily, Mazie would push, hit, or scream to get her way. Observing that aggression was so often used to gain an objective, Robin concluded that the child had established an entrenched pattern of instrumental aggression. Mazie believed that the only way to feel safe in her environment was by controlling it.

Whenever Mazie experienced a total outburst, endangering others and herself, Robin used the passive bear hug. Mazie fought her whenever she used this calming procedure, but she would eventually calm down, and the two would then sit together and perhaps read a book. Robin did her best to let Mazie know why she was using this technique through quiet talks before and after conflicts. Mazie was a tough kid, and Robin had the bruises to prove it, but she and the staff were committed to staying with the child.

Robin followed center policy for documenting the conflicts. As soon as she realized that Mazie's extreme instrumental aggression was continuing, Robin and her team held an IGP meeting with the parents. Robin correctly figured that because of the circumstances regarding how Mazie began in the program, the family would want to cooperate in forming a strategy to help her stay.

At the meeting, Robin started with positive comments about Mazie's presence in the group, then shared the pattern of behavior and explained that her job was to help Mazie have an easier time getting along. Robin explained how the staff was intentionally building positive relationships with Mazie. She explained how they used positive guidance at school and encouraged Mazie's parents to try a similar approach at home. The family approved of the measures, and the adults came up with a plan that they all felt comfortable with. Robin was pleased (and relieved) that Mazie's parents were willing to work together with her.

Robin, the late-shift teacher Joyce, and two teacher assistants met with Iris, the center director, to make the IGP operational in the learning setting. Each staff member would spend quality one-on-one time with Mazie each day to build trusting relationships. Robin, who despite all got along well with Mazie, took the lead in this effort. During times when Mazie experienced more difficulties, one of the two teacher assistants would shadow Mazie and help her avoid and de-escalate conflicts. Robin and Mazie's parents agreed that if Mazie had three incidents in one day, Robin and Mazie would call Mazie's dad. Mazie seemed upset when the calls were made, more so than Robin expected. Robin did not want to add to Mazie's stress level, so she eased up on the phone calls and concentrated on using her relationship with the child to teach behavioral alternatives.

Each day, outside of the conflicts, Robin and the assistant teachers made a point of having contact talks with Mazie. These contact talks let her know that the adults really cared about her and that preschool was a place to learn how to make friends and get along with others. They actively coached Mazie about how to play with other children and how to ask for things she wanted. Guidance talks were almost as numerous as the contact talks each day, and the staff worked hard to keep the guidance talks friendly, while still being firm with Mazie about limits. During conflict mediations, Robin and Joyce often put an arm around Mazie's shoulders, keeping Mazie away from the other child. They always gave Mazie time and assistance in settling down before starting mediation. They made a point of having Mazie hear from the other child about the conflict. They used the other children's words to teach Mazie what she needed to say and do in order to get along with her mates.

As the year continued, Robin saw that the plan seemed to be working. Mazie had fewer conflicts and made progress in expressing her needs positively. In follow-up meetings, her parents were clearly grateful for the progress, and both Mom and Dad said they were spending more one-on-one quality time with her at home. As she progressed in managing her aggression, Mazie was becoming a leader among the children in a variety of activities, an attribute that did not surprise Robin. But the child still had a way to go.

Here is how the teaching team led by Robin, director Iris, and mother Sylvia used the seven steps in implementing a comprehensive guidance plan for Mazie:

1. Observe and record pattern of mistaken behavior.
Robin and Joyce couldn't miss the conflicts that Mazie caused when she started in the program. They recorded observations of the outbursts on the program's anecdotal observation forms and filed them with director Iris. The three discussed the observations, which helped Robin realize that they were seeing a pattern of instrumental aggression. They decided they needed to observe times when Iris was not having problems—almost always when she was playing alone or with others, using materials in the ways that she wanted.

Robin observed that the other children usually gave in to Mazie's demands out of fear of her retaliation. Robin reflected that the teachers felt like doing the same! From her journal: "It is a daily challenge to always be close by to intercede and help ensure a safe and happy environment for the other children. I have noticed that the other children are becoming leery of her and keep their distance."

2. Build the relationships.
The staff developed attitudes about Mazie; some found themselves less than eager to have contact talks with her. Robin encouraged them to have the talks. The child's instrumental aggression was a symptom of insecurity relative to basic needs (like the need for secure relationships with adults), causing Mazie to feel toxic stress that she acted out in relation to through her intentional aggression. Robin felt that holding an IGP meeting early in the year would, among other things, spur (or at least nudge) the staff into having one-on-one time with Mazie daily.

As to the parents, Robin was aware that they were a bit desperate after having their child expelled from the first program. The family knew Iris and some of the other staff persons at Robin's center from their daughter Emma's time in the program. The staff knew the parents to be sincere if sometimes distant and inconsistent in their parenting styles. Although not outgoing with Robin, the parents did seem keenly interested in having Mazie get along in her setting. Robin counted on this in figuring the parents would come to an IGP meeting and perhaps follow through on a plan.

3. Use consistent guidance intervention techniques.

At the beginning, the four staff members working (the two shifts) with Mazie's group were not all on the same page regarding which methods to use. Time constraints made staffing difficult; they communicated with each other about Mazie, but mainly on the run. Robin and director Iris were aware of this. They agreed that formalizing an IGP would bring the staff and the parents to the table so that needed discussion, planning, and coordination could occur.

4. Obtain additional information.

Robin used her good professional relationship with director Iris to discuss Mazie's situation. Robin was deeply troubled by Mazie's lack of caring about others' feelings. Some children need intensive assistance in building the empathy that comes so naturally to others. This is due in part to their brain neuroarchitecture—how their brains form and operate (Weber et al. 2008).

But Robin also thought that trauma in Mazie's life had breached a basic sense of trust and caused her to react with intention to a world she saw as confrontational. Mazie apparently had a negative experience in her previous program—the victim of bullying the first year and neglected the next. Robin commented, "I am sure that Mazie wasn't oblivious to why she left the family child care program, whatever the effect this 'failure' might have had on her. Moreover, she may have been rankled by being the bratty younger sister of Emma, a child regarded as sweet." With the switch in providers, Mazie clearly saw elements of the new program as threatening.

5. Hold IGP meeting.

The parents arrived early for the IGP meeting. After greetings and compliment sandwiches about how Mazie was doing, the staff and parents discussed the behaviors they all would target. They introduced the concept of mistaken behavior to the parents, explaining that Mazie was showing level three mistaken behavior.

Robin used the meeting to introduce and discuss the guidance techniques they would use: contact talks, prevention measures, calming techniques, guidance talks, and high-level conflict mediation. The two teacher assistants would coordinate their overlapping work schedules so that either could shadow Mazie at times when she was prone to outbursts. Robin would be in close contact with Iris, who would let any floating staff members know about the situation. Robin would take the lead with conflict intervention most of the day, and Joyce would take over after

Robin left; this would provide Mazie with as much continuity as they could during times when the child was experiencing difficulties.

Regarding the family, the group agreed to try a phone call to a parent if Mazie had three strong conflicts in a day. It was the father's idea that they should call him. Robin suggested that the family have regular dedicated contact talks with Mazie each day (quality one-on-one time) in addition to reading to her each night (also opportunities for contact talks).

Iris was big on a parent doing a regular fun activity with a child outside the home each week (a parent-child date), and Robin made this suggestion. Though both parents worked, they said they would give this a try. Robin and Sylvia, the mother, set a date to discuss coordination of guidance techniques during conflicts between the program and home. (Robin wanted to encourage Sylvia to try techniques other than frequent time-outs in Mazie's room.) The family appreciated that Robin and the staff were there to help their daughter, and they agreed to do as much as they could on their end as well.

The staff-parent team set a day for a follow-up meeting in three weeks.

6. Implement guidance plan.

Robin felt that the staff was now taking a coordinated approach toward Mazie by way of building relations and intervening consistently in conflicts. Each staff member had contact talks with Mazie every day. Outside of the conflict-related guidance talks, they often managed to work in a little free advice about what Mazie might and might not do to have kids want to play with her. The two teacher assistants used their shadow times to continue providing Mazie with firm but friendly structure.

Robin met with Sylvia. The two talked about the guidance interventions the staff was using. They also discussed why Mazie might be bothered about having to call Dad. Sylvia relayed that the father's style was to ignore Mazie's mistaken behavior until he lost it, then yell at her and send her to her room. Robin shared that things were getting better with Mazie, and the phone calls weren't proving necessary.

6. Monitor guidance plan.

Anecdotal observations done by the staff documented that Mazie had gone from an average of three outbursts a day during the first two weeks to three a week by the time of the follow-up IGP meeting. And, encouragingly, the conflicts were more verbal and less physical now. Mazie was still working on using nonhurting words during conflicts, just as many children, and some adults (like Mazie's father) have to. The staff concluded that although Mazie still had dramatic outbursts over issues of property, territory, and privilege, she was making progress with DLS 1 and 2. Her status in the group was not in question—this program would not ask the child to leave. There had been significant bonding between Mazie and a few of the staff persons. Mazie seemed much more comfortable with herself and the program. She did not need to assert her will on others nearly as much as when she began.

All this was discussed in the second IGP meeting in mid-October. The parents reported that they were seeing progress with the measures they were taking at home, as well. (Sylvia later shared with Robin that Dad was yelling less and finding more things to do with his daughters.) In the year and a half before Mazie began kindergarten, the staff became more able to enjoy Mazie's pluckiness, leadership, and grit. The staff shared a faith that their hard work at using guidance during this time would show in Mazie's behavior into the future.

Notes about Comprehensive Guidance

The two case studies provide illustrations of how comprehensive guidance works using the Individual Guidance Plan and meetings. Teachers who initiate and follow through with this sometimes complicated process are indeed guidance professionals who are practicing liberation teaching. They are not giving up on children in need. In the following notes, I offer some further considerations for using comprehensive guidance. I hope these comments are useful to you.

Reactive and Instrumental Aggression

Chronic stress leads to both reactive and instrumental aggression. The most straightforward form is reactive aggression, which Eduardo predominantly showed in his vignette. Reactive aggression is a reflexive, amygdala-driven fight reaction when a child perceives a threat, real or imagined. If a child would sit too closely to Eduardo, for instance, he would use hands and feet to (in his view) fend off the child. His state of mind made the boy prone to reactive aggression. The child sitting too closely was the trigger. Cora's effort was to build a trust-based relationship with Eduardo to help him manage his stress and see situations as less threatening. As a result, over time, Eduardo found reactive aggression less necessary, and when he did express it, he did so in less hurting ways.

Instrumental aggression is a learned response that becomes a coping strategy for the child. The intentional nature of instrumental aggression makes it particularly challenging for teachers. Fair-minded early childhood teachers understandably have a hard time with the injustices children like Mazie inflict on others. After all, "She did it on purpose." In all her years as a teacher, Robin could not recall a child who showed more instrumental aggression than Mazie. In working with children like Mazie, teachers may be tempted to let things go and mark off days on the calendar, or discipline strictly to shame the child into being good—an ineffective and discredited practice. As Mazie and her family experienced, when providers run out of patience and ideas, the ultimate punishment too often is expulsion. The challenge for teachers is that young children who do not learn alternative strategies to instrumental aggression may suffer long-term emotional and social problems (Kaiser and Sklar Rasminksy 2016). Robin did not acquiesce to the inevitability of neurology in Mazie. She used the resources she could bring to the situation and worked on a collaborative approach to provide true liberation teaching for this child. Her goal was to model and teach empathy.

The Opposite of Aggression

Psychologists have commented to me that, for the child, freeze and flee survival responses are every bit as serious as reactive and instrumental fight responses. I think this statement is true especially in mass-class situations in K–12 programs. In classes of twenty or more, children can engage in freeze and subtle flee reactions to become invisible students. At the extremes, these kids tend to isolate themselves or blend in to be inconspicuous, doing what they need to not stand out in any way. Any bit of attention or task expectation from a teacher is scary to these kids. A sobering example of this invisible child syndrome is a mother who conveyed the following frustration to me after a parent-teacher conference. During the conference, the teacher failed to comment about or even recognize that the parent's child had missed two weeks of third grade with a serious case of the flu!

Becoming invisible is a way some children cope with stress. Building supportive relationships with these children while they are young is crucial to help them gain DLS 1 and 2 so they can blossom—whether like violets or peonies. (Individual differences really do blossom when children are able to work on DLS 3, 4, and 5, a very cool thing about encouraging early learning communities.)

Adults do not need teaching degrees to build helping relationships with super-quiet children. But it sure helps to have small group sizes. In many states, mandated adult-child ratios make these relationships generally easier in preschool settings than in elementary classrooms. When family child care providers can afford not to have an overload of children, they, too, can build all-important proactive positive relationships. Guidance practices are so much easier when group sizes (and teacher stress levels) are manageable. I say down with the mass-class phenomenon!

Work with Outside Professionals

Some children are resilient in the face of personal traumas that might deeply harm others (Cairone 2016). In most children, chronic stress dampens social responsiveness while at the same time boosting the fight-or-flight reaction. These happenings make the child vulnerable to the stress-rejection cycle (Gunnar, Herrera, and Hostinar 2009). Gilliam and Shahar (2006) state that nationally, about 8 percent of all preschoolers (children age three to five years) exhibit behavioral problems severe enough to warrant a psychiatric diagnosis. Other studies indicate this number is much greater, especially in communities with high levels of poverty (Cairone 2016).

As part of comprehensive guidance, with the family's permission, outside professionals can be enlisted for assessments and special services for the child and family. As well outside professionals can provide staff with information, consultation, and support. In the first case study involving Eduardo, a trained teacher from the school district did a special-needs screening for the child and recommended a follow-up assessment. (In all states, school districts are required by federal law to do screenings and assessments for children at least as young as three years old.)

Other clinics and treatment centers—including Head Start—do assessments and provide more comprehensive services than child care programs typically can. Early childhood professionals do well to know workers in community agencies that they and their families can contact and cooperatively work with. Either in person or through reports, outside professionals are often helpful resources in follow-up IGP meetings.

Again, family members have achieved the second level of engagement to feel comfortable with using professionals from outside the care and education program. When parents have reached the second level, they will often accept referrals for parenting classes, special programs for their children, and family and child counseling, as well as support services for nutrition, housing, education, and employment needs. Many beneficial family services become possible because of growing trust between the early childhood professional and family members. When teachers know and can make referrals to familiar professionals at community support services, they fully extend service possibilities to their families.

Difficult Considerations

When a child inflicts obvious harm on others, especially on a continuing basis, teachers are faced with difficult considerations that might extend beyond the usual IGP process.

One consideration is whether to have a group meeting with the children themselves to help them understand (a) the behaviors of the child causing conflicts and (b) actions group members can take, if necessary. An example in chapter 5 is the meeting where the professionals taught the toddler group to defend themselves against biting. Other examples can be found in chapter 8, "Guidance Leadership with the Group," of my textbook, *A Guidance Approach for the Encouraging Classroom.* One must take particular care in these meetings to protect the dignity of the child at the center of the conflicts.

A second consideration is whether to meet with family members of the other children in the group, some of whom may have been the objects of level three mistaken behavior by the child. Providers should especially consider such a meeting if they notice that parents are beginning to talk about the conflicts. While respecting the privacy of individual children and families, teachers meet with parents to help them understand the program's guidance policy and the steps the staff is taking to ensure safety. These meetings need to be dialogues—staff members talking with, not at, parents—so that family members can express concerns and gain understanding. One father's attitude softened when he recalled that he, too, had shown aggression in his early years at school. The challenges of such meetings are an important reason why the teacher builds relations with families when they first enter the program.

Meetings with other parents are especially difficult for family members of the child causing the conflicts. These family members should always be informed in advance of the meeting, perhaps in the solutions part of an IGP meeting. They should be reassured that privacy will be strictly maintained, and usually they should be given the option of attending. The lead teacher should explain that just as the staff wants this family's child to say in the program, they want other parents to know they are ensuring safety so their children can also stay. Meetings with the other parents are never fun, and they are not automatically held, but they might prove necessary in certain situations.

A third consideration is this: there might come a time when teachers realize a child is so entrenched in survival behaviors that his or her needs go beyond the resources of their program. Liberation teaching means never giving up on a child, but sometimes that commitment means the child should leave for another setting that has more resources. Guidance professionals consider this conclusion only after they give their all to comprehensive guidance and the steps of the IGP. Helping the family find a better-equipped program is important. Easing the transition lets the family know that the present staff has been on their side from beginning to end. This understanding alone may be enough for a family to buffer a challenged child against falling into the stress-rejection cycle.

Comprehensive guidance, even with the use of the IGP, seldom results in a storybook ending. When they use the process, early childhood professionals usually see improvement more than transformation. Even if the outcome is less than perfect, teachers realize the following benefits: they feel less consternation about the child, and they are more understanding; they feel less worry for other children in the program and feel more capable of handling conflicts that do arise; and they feel less concern about the family's reactions to the staff and feel more connection with the family—a mutual acceptance that they are on the same team. Perhaps most important, teachers feel more confident about a positive future for the child.

In his 2005 and 2006 studies, Walter Gilliam identifies a systemic problem in working with children who show repeated serious conflicts. Early childhood care and education programs need the active assistance of mental health and behavior interventionist professionals. A few states have made some efforts to establish such resources, and Head Start has done so on the national level. Still, except in particular community situations (as in Eduardo's story), the assistance of mental health professionals in education—including school district services to children in preschool programs—needs to become a higher national priority.

From Survival to Resilience

Liberation teaching is not giving up on any child. It means moving out of one's comfort zone to learn about the child and family, building positive relationships with both, and teaching the child the abilities of resilience—managing stress, building relations with others, and expressing emotions in nonhurting ways. If, after exhaustive tries at comprehensive guidance, the child is not making progress with DLS 1 and 2, the early childhood professional works with the family to find a setting for the child with more guidance resources. Such referrals mark the difference between expulsion and working to find a more effective placement for the child. Only when the child leaves the program, hopefully via the referral, does the early childhood professional let go of the child, knowing she or he has done all that can be done.

There is no question that early childhood professionals are underpaid and undervalued in this society. Professionals who stay in the field, practice guidance, and work closely with families are, for this author, as close to being angelic as we humans can become. They are liberating teachers who every day help children living at a survival level move toward resiliency. Every day, they change young children's lives for the better in lifelong ways. Through their efforts, our society can and will make it to the next century.

I hope that this book has been readable, meaningful, and useful to you. Since I'm from Minnesota, let's move on with the words of the great American Garrison Keillor: "Nothing you do for children is ever wasted."

Discussion Questions

1. What seems to you to be the main challenges in building relationships with children who are showing level three mistaken behavior? Discuss strategies for dealing with these challenges.

2. What seems to you to be the main challenges in building relationships with family members? Discuss strategies for dealing with these challenges.

3. What seems to you to be the main challenges in building relationships with fellow staff members? Discuss strategies for dealing with these challenges.

4. Accomplishing liberation teaching is something most developing professionals aspire to. Discuss some steps you can take in your development that can help you progress toward using liberation teaching in your work.

Key Concepts

Definitions of the Key Concepts can be found in the glossary on pages 177–84.

Buffering

Childhood post-traumatic stress syndrome

Comprehensive guidance

Resiliency/Being resilient

Appendix

Glossary of Key Concepts

Anti-bias education: "An approach to early childhood education that sets forth values-based principles and methodology in support of respecting and embracing differences and acting against bias and unfairness." (Teaching for Change 2016)

Attachment theory: Explains how adult-child relationships impacts the psychological development of the child during the first few years.

Authentic assessment: A practice that uses samples of the child's everyday work and efforts to assess the child's progress on a developmental continuum.

Buffering: Building and sustaining a caring relationship with and an encouraging environment for a child who is experiencing toxic stress in order to help the child feel a sense of worth and belonging and to progress toward resilience.

Cardinal principle: Haim Ginott's guidance fundamental that holds that when teachers become upset, they focus on the situation and preserve the worth and dignity of the child.

Childhood post-traumatic stress syndrome: Suffered by children who are overcome by toxic stress due to traumatic experiences that result in extreme survival behaviors.

Collaboration: Two or more adults working together cooperatively to accomplish goals and solve problems more easily than an individual acting alone.

Compliment sandwich: A communication technique intended to sustain relationships by sandwiching a leader's concerns between two (better yet three) compliments about the other's progress, strengths, and/or achievements.

Comprehensive guidance: The intentional integration of a mix of guidance practices—including collaboration with families, other staff members, and professionals—to help children build trusting relationships, manage toxic stress, and learn nonhurting ways of expressing strong emotions; to gain DLS 1 and 2 and make progress with DLS 3, 4, and 5, thus gaining resilience.

Conflict management: The skills of social problem solving that we want children (all humans?) to learn; the ability to prevent and de-escalate conflicts through the use of nonhurting words.

Conflict mediation: The method used by a third party (usually, but not necessarily, an adult) to teach children involved in a serious conflict to de-escalate and resolve the conflict in nonhurting ways.

Conflicts: Expressed disagreements between individuals. Conflicts are a part of everyday human experience.

Contact talk: A quality-time conversation that allows the parties to learn more about one another and build a trusting relationship. Distinct from "task talks," which are held to get tasks completed.

Cooling-down time: The time and space a teacher gives children to help them calm down after a conflict to make calm discussion about the conflict possible.

Cultural competence: To be cognitively and socially responsive (ethical and intelligent) toward members of the early childhood community who may be different than you physically, ethnically, culturally, religiously, and/or linguistically; the ability to accommodate social and cultural uniqueness in the daily program.

Describe, express, direct: When intervening in a conflict a three-part strategy of describing what you see, expressing how you feel, and directing children to alternative behaviors. A practice popularized by Haim Ginott to help the adult address the problem rather than criticize the child or children involved in the conflict.

Developmentally appropriate practice: Curriculum and teaching practices that are responsive to the levels, patterns, and cultural circumstances of development in each child in a group.

Dual-language learners: Learners in the process of gaining command of a second language, either English, if the home language is a different language, or another language if the home language is English.

Educational meetings: Group meetings held by the teacher with children to cooperatively plan, revise, and review group learning activities and projects.

Encouraging learning community: A developmentally appropriate environment that empowers each child to feel a sense of belonging to the group and confidence in the learning process.

Executive functions: The coordinated functions centered in the frontal cortex that enable individuals to bring memory, reasoning ability, and persistence to bear in addressing tasks and challenges. The executive function process is in a state of development from age three into adulthood and is undermined by unmanageable stress.

Experimentation mistaken behavior (level one): The level of mistaken behavior during conflicts that indicates that individuals are meeting safety needs and can encounter their environments openly, even if with mistakes in judgment.

Family groups: Stable small groups in the early childhood community, often having mixed ages of children. Family groups have primary caregivers and do activities together, like meals, rest, specific activities, and reading stories.

Five democratice life skills: Goals of guidance and indices of psychological-social health in the individual.

The first two survival skills involve finding acceptance by others and expressing strong emotions in nonhurting ways. The three growth skills that follow entail creative problem-solving, accepting human differences, and acting ethically and intelligently.

Five-finger formula for conflict mediation:

Thumb: Calm everyone involved.

Pointer: Come to agreement on how each child sees the conflict.

Tall guy: Brainstorm possible ways to resolve the conflict.

Ringer: All agree to solution and implement it.

Pinky: Adult monitors and acknowledges children's efforts and holds a guidance talk with one or more children separately to reinforce the process.

Friendly humor: Humor shared between individuals that affirms relationships through the light-hearted interpretation of everyday experiences.

Group guidelines: Guidelines that children and teachers establish together to guide group meetings; the personal guidelines that teachers have as reminders for how to facilitate and lead group meetings.

Group meetings: Meetings held in center-based and family child care programs, Head Starts, and other early childhood classrooms for the purpose of building and maintaining an inclusive and cooperative encouraging learning community.

Guidance: Developmentally appropriate teaching in the emotional and social domains; the use of professional leadership to teach for healthy emotional and social development in all children of the learning community.

Guidance talk: Conversation that an adult holds with children around conflicts that informally follows the five-finger formula in order to resolve problems, teach reconciliation, and guide toward nonhurting alternative behaviors for "next time."

High-level mediation: Teachers use the five-finger formula in a direct manner by calming, using firm but friendly leadership, and actively coaching children who need teacher assistance to resolve a conflict.

I-messages: A technique that teachers use selectively to express strong emotions in a relatively nonhurting manner—in contrast to disparaging you-messages.

Instrumental aggression: Amygdala-driven learning in which the child uses aggression intentionally as a mistaken strategy to finding safety and security.

Level three day: A terrible, no good, very bad day, which can happen to anyone, adult or child, once in a while.

Levels of family engagement: The levels of family involvement within the early childhood community:

> **One:** Acceptance of program information
>
> **Two:** Active educational engagement with one's child
>
> **Three:** Active program participation
>
> **Four:** Personal/professional development

A suggested goal for early childhood settings is to have all parents attain at least level two.

Liberation teaching: The intentional guidance practice of not giving up on a child. This highest form of guidance pertains particularly to the adult's leadership with children showing level three mistaken behavior and who may be vulnerable to rejection and stigma by the group.

Low-level mediation: Teachers use the five-finger formula as a facilitator rather than a coach; through teacher cues and verbal support, children take ownership in the conflict-mediation process.

Mastery learning: When young children are empowered to utilize mastery (intrinsic) motivation, they engage with interesting materials and activities wholeheartedly. If this engagement allows the child to have a full and extensive experience, perhaps over time, the result is mastery learning.

Mastery motivation: The natural internal motivation in each human to learn and grow psychologically. Mastery motivation can only manifest itself when children are relatively free of the stress of perceived threat, including in the learning setting.

Melting Pot theory: The widely held attitude that the role of schools was to socialize immigrants and minority-group children to American ideas and values. In the past, education policy makers strictly adhered to Melting Pot theory, to the detriment of the identities of minority group families. Under this policy, children often come to feel torn between the cultural influences of home and school.

Mistaken behavior: The conflicts that children cause or fall into that result in potential or actual harm and serious disruption; mistakes in judgment that escalate conflicts to the point of harm and disruption.

Open-ended meetings: Group meetings held by the teacher with the group to civilly discuss hypothetical and real-life situations that affect or might affect the encouraging learning community. Talks can be philosophical in nature at the children's level.

Passive bear hug: The calming technique of last resort when a child has totally lost emotional control and there is an immediate danger of harm to the child and/ or others. The teacher goes into a sitting position and holds the child facing away with head out to one side. The adult sings, whispers, or remains quiet until the child realizes that the adult is helping her or him regain control and subsequently calms down. The PBH is used only within the context of the state's and program's written policies.

Peer negotiation: The process used by two or a few children involved in a conflict to de-escalate and resolve the conflict peaceably by themselves; evidence that children have achieved a key guidance goal through learning and using the basics of conflict management.

Perspective taking: Engaging in practical empathy for another—understanding the other's viewpoints and feelings—to solve mutual social problems.

Power of silence: The psychological pull on persons in authority to say and do nothing when they see a person or persons in their charge oppressing another; failing to use liberation teaching out of a fear of doing or saying something wrong.

Privilege conflict: A conflict over who gets a perceived privilege.

Proactive positive relationships: Using one's leadership as a professional from the very first day to form and maintain a secure attachment with the child in the learning setting.

Problem-solving meetings: Group meetings held by the teacher to civilly discuss and resolve public issues and problems that are affecting the encouraging learning community.

Property conflict: A conflict over the ownership of property.

Reactive aggression: Impulsive lashing out when a child feels a real or imagined threat; the reactive survival behavior of agression, which is most challenging for caring adults to address.

Reciprocal relationships: Relationships built by early childhood professionals with members of children's families in which each partner feels empowered toward cooperation on behalf of the child.

Reconciliation: The important way to bring closure to conflicts so that child and teacher are both gaining practice in the five democratic life skills.

Reflective listening: The supportive acknowledgment of the verbal and nonverbal communications of the child. Reflective listening tells children that the teacher cares and that what the child feels matters.

Resiliency/Being resilient: The state of mind when a child previously at risk gains a sense of individual worth and belonging, has made progress with expressing strong feelings in nonhurting ways, and is responding to new situations creatively and cooperatively. The child has been helped to attain DLS 1 and 2 and is progressing with DLS 3, 4, and 5.

Scaffolding: The interaction pattern in which one individual uses perspective taking to flexibly assist another to increase knowledge and understanding in a way that person could not accomplish independently.

Secure attachments: Sustained relationships between children and primary adults that meet the child's needs for safety, love, and belonging, thus empowering healthy emotional and social development by the child.

Self-removal: An intermediate goal in guiding children to manage strong emotions. Instead of falling deeper into a conflict, children leave the conflict scene on their own.

Self-report: Honestly communicating from the standpoint of personal perceptions rather than through blanket judgments and name-calling. Child example: "I am upset that you are squeezing my arm. Stop it!" Adult example: "I am bothered by the hitting I see. Please sit on these two chairs, and we will get calm."

Significant learning: Learning that stays with the child long after the specific experience and motivates the child to have similar experiences in the future. Significant learning means that the emotional dimension of the original learning experience was positive, motivating the child toward, and not away from, related learning experiences to follow.

Socially influenced mistaken behavior (level two): The level of mistaken behavior during conflicts that indicates the individual has partially met safety needs and finds security in following the lead of more powerful individuals; going along to get along in conflict situations.

Story pictures: Pictures children make that tell stories, which adults do well to encourage. Story pictures are part of a creative arts program that leads to progress in children's capacity for self-expression on paper, moving from preschematic to creatively conventional representation during early childhood.

Stress-rejection cycle: The unfortunate, potentially long-term social-psychological cycle that too many children who experience toxic stress fall into. The cycle develops when young children feel toxic stress; show aggression as a mistaken behavior to relieve the stress; experience negative attention, punishment, and rejection as a result of the conflict; and feel anger, shame, and personal debasement as a result of the punishment and rejection—which further adds to the toxic stress and reinforces the behavior pattern.

Survival (strong unmet needs) mistaken behavior (level three): The level of mistaken behavior during conflicts that indicates the individual has strong unmet needs for safety, security, and a sense of belonging. The unmet needs cause toxic stress in the individual, which he or she tries to alleviate through mistaken survival behaviors that tend to be serious and repeated.

Teacher: An adult in the learning and care setting who has leadership responsibilities with children. This broad definition suits the purpose of this book to especially include child care providers in homes and centers, some of whom may be a child's primary teacher outside the home throughout the early years.

Teaching team: A differentiated staffing arrangement in early childhood care and education programs where persons of different backgrounds, qualifications, and levels of experience work together as a team. The lead teacher builds mutually appreciative relations with these other adults—assistant teachers, parent volunteers, student teachers—for the good of every child in the program.

Territory conflict: A conflict over the occupation of space.

Three levels of mistaken behavior: The construct that connects levels of mental health with characteristic mistaken behaviors that children at each of the three levels show during conflicts. The construct objectively demonstrates how mistaken behavior includes not just innocent mistakes, but acts done on purpose.

Toxic stress: Stress due to environmental and/or physiological challenges that is sufficiently high as to be unmanageable by the stressed individual—young children are particularly susceptible to toxic stress.

Individual Guidance Plan Worksheet

Child's name: _____ Child's age: _____ Initial Write-up date: _____
(years and months)

1. Noted Behaviors

Behaviors observed: Thoughts about Behaviors:

_____   _____

_____   _____

_____   _____

2. Additional Information

Check procedures used. Then summarize information gained.

❏ Discussion with child   Date: _____   ❏ Discussion with other staff   Date: _____

❏ Discussion with parent   Date: _____   ❏ Discussion with other professionals   Date: _____

Summary:

_____

_____

_____

3. Individual Guidance Plan Meeting   Date: _____

Persons attending meeting:

_____

_____

_____

Summary of strategies to be tried:

_____

_____

_____

4. Follow-Up Meeting or Review   Date: _____

Effort/progress shown by child:

_____

_____

_____

Progress still needed:

_____

_____

_____

Any changes in plan:

_____

_____

_____

5. Summary of Results and Any Changes in IGP as of (First Date)

_____

_____

_____

6. Summary of Results and Any Changes in IGP as of (Second Date)

_____

_____

_____

7. Final Summary of Results, Exit Meeting (If Held), and Future Actions

_____

_____

_____

The IGP document is adapted from the *Instructor's Manual for A Guidance Approach for the Encouraging Classroom*, 5th edition (2010) by Dan Gartrell. Thanks to publisher Wadsworth/Cengage for making this material available.

Resources by Dan Gartrell

Annotated List of Guidance Matters Columns in *Young Children*

Thanks to permission from NAEYC, free downloads of the columns are available at www.dangartrell.net.

November 2005, "DAP: The Heart of Guidance." This first column illustrates how a child care staff makes their program developmentally appropriate for a three-year-old. The column argues that *guidance* (teaching young children to learn from their mistakes and to solve their problems) requires developmentally appropriate practice.

January 2006, "Jeremiah." In the face of a large study on preschool expulsion, this column illustrates how teachers can accept the challenge of challenging behaviors and build positive relationships. Six communication techniques that help build relationships and guide behavior are explained.

March 2006, "A Student Teacher Uses Conflict Mediation." In her preschool student teaching, Kelly uses conflict mediation with success. The column analyzes why her effort succeeded, offers five steps that teach mediation, and identifies mediation potholes to avoid.

May 2006, "Boys and Men Teachers." Vignettes illustrate how two men teachers built relationships with boys having problems. Their breakthroughs illustrate the importance of including men teachers in early childhood classrooms.

July 2006, "A Spoonful of Laughter." Examples illustrate the use of humor to de-escalate conflicts, aid in guidance interventions, and put children at ease in stressful situations. "If anything goes exactly as you expect with young children, something is wrong."

September 2006, "Building Relationships through Talk." As teachers and young children get to know each other through contact talks, trust builds and classroom conflicts decrease. The column emphasizes having contact talks especially when at-risk children first arrive in the classroom.

November 2006, "The Beauty of Class Meetings." Class meetings affirm that the group is encouraging for all. Meetings at different age levels are illustrated; guidelines for the meetings are provided. Meetings are alternatives to old-fashioned group punishment. (See also January 2012 column.)

January 2007, "Tattling: It Drives Teachers Bonkers!" The title says it all, so what can a teacher do? The column offers reasons for tattling and creative responses to it. Teachers can learn to handle tattling in ways that teach children vital life lessons.

March 2007, "Competition: What Part in Our Programs?" For reasons of limited experience and still-developing brains, losing makes young children feel inadequate and unworthy. Teachers prepare young children for future competition by deemphasizing winning and losing and guiding them to successfully participate.

May 2007, "'You Really Worked Hard on Your Picture': Guiding with Encouragement." The column explores an alternative to traditional praise: giving encouragement. The key to encouragement, complimenting details and listening, acknowledges that the teacher really cares.

September 2007, "He Did it On Purpose!" Punishment diminishes self-esteem, raises stress levels, and can start self-fulfilling prophecies. The column explores reasons children cause conflicts and suggests guidance responses that teach rather than punish.

November 2007, "Swearing and Words That Hurt." The column explores three motivations for why children use hurting words: experimentation, the influence of others, and unmet needs. Discussed are techniques that guide children to express emotions in nonhurting ways.

January 2008, "Comprehensive Guidance." An experienced teacher builds relationships with a child and his mother. When the child's conflicts escalate, the teacher maintains the relationships, provides firm but friendly guidance, and facilitates the family's participation in therapy.

March 2008, "Promote Physical Activity. It's Proactive Guidance." Quiet classrooms undermine the development of active children. The column references and discusses techniques that integrate movement with learning activity and that make the classroom encouraging for all.

May 2008, "Understand Bullying." Behind every act of bullying is a child with a difficult life. Learning about children who bully helps the teacher build an encouraging classroom for all; bullying then becomes unnecessary. Extensive resource list is included.

March 2011, "Children Who Have Serious Conflicts, Part One." Part one addresses reactive aggression, when children feel threatened and act out to protect themselves. Illustrated is how a teacher works with reactive aggression due to high stress in the child's life.

July 2011, "Children Who Have Serious Conflicts, Part Two." Part two discusses instrumental aggression, when children use aggression to impose their wills on others to gain a personal objective. The column addresses this most challenging problem.

November 2011, "Aggression, the Prequel: Reducing the Need." A teacher uses comprehensive guidance with a toddler to build an attachment and keep reactive aggression from becoming instrumental. Firm but friendly limits, cuddling, choices, and parent relations prove effective.

January 2012, "From Rules to Guidelines: Moving to the Positive. Rules tend to be stated in the negative and set up negative expectations in children's and teachers' minds. Moving to the positive through guidelines, teachers are able to guide, not just punish, when children have conflicts.

May 2012, "'Goodest' Guidance: Teachers and Families Together." The column profiles a Head Start parent and her home visitor and the results of their six-year collaboration. The parent's gains across four levels of engagement are reflected in good service delivery for her children.

September 2012, "Democratic Life Skill One: Guiding Children to Find a Place." The column is the first in a series of five on teaching for the democratic life skills (DLS). By building healthy relationships, the teacher helps the child find a place of acceptance in the group as a worthy individual.

March 2013, "Democratic Life Skill Two: Expressing Strong Emotions in Non-Hurting Ways." Second of five columns on the DLS. Through maintaining healthy relationships by using guidance practices during conflicts, teachers assist children with gaining DLS 2.

July 2013, "Democratic Life Skill Three: Solving Problems Creatively." This column explores practices that empower the capacity to solve problems independently and with others. Three vignettes provide the basis for exploring how young children show DLS 3.

November 2013, "Democratic Life Skill Four: Accepting Unique Human Qualities in Others." This fourth column on the DLS examines two vignettes that illustrate young children who show accepting behaviors and discusses how to nurture these behaviors.

March 2014, "Democratic Life Skill Five: Acting Intelligently and Ethically." Two vignettes focus on one child who is beginning to make progress toward DLS 5 and one child who teaches adults about DLS in a difficult social situation. End of series on DLS.

July 2014, "Fostering Resilience: Teaching Emotional-Social Skills." (Cowritten with Karen Cairone) This case study illustrates how a behavioral consultant worked collaboratively with an early childhood education staff and a child's mother to guide the child to cope with his toxic stress, build trust with significant adults, and make progress in selected emotional-social skills.

November 2014, "Guidance with Girls." (Cowritten with Layna Cole) Teacher Maya uses firm but friendly guidance to help Charlene join boy firefighters in active role play. The staff follows up with emergent curricula, including group meetings, featured books, and a visit from a woman firefighter in order to guide girls and boys toward gender inclusivity.

Media Resources

Web chat: July 2011. The Goals of Good Guidance: Understanding and Responding to Challenging Behaviors. Online chat with Dan.

An Afternoon with the Experts: Dan Gartrell on Guidance (DVD)
NAEYC Online Store
Multimedia: Item #8206
Learning what good guidance is and how to use it effectively with young children is the most important—and often the most difficult—part of working with young children. In this DVD, Dan Gartrell clarifies what effective guidance looks like, tells how to provide it in classrooms, and explains why providing good guidance for children is imperative for their lifelong social and emotional success. From Chattahoochee Technical College.

Resources by Redleaf Press

Beyond Behavior Management: The Six Life Skills Children Need, Second Edition, by Jenna Bilmes

Bridging the Relationship Gap: Connecting with Children Facing Adversity by Sara E. Langworthy

Caring for Young Children with Special Needs by Cindy Croft

Cultivating the Genius of Black Children by Debra Ren-Etta Sullivan

Discovering the Culture of Childhood by Emily Plank

Doing the Right Thing for Children: Eight Qualities of Leadership by Maurice Sykes

Embracing Rough-and-Tumble Play: Teaching with the Body in Mind by Mike Huber

From Parents to Partners: Building a Family-Centered Early Childhood Program, Second Edition, by Janis Keyser

The Great Disconnect in Early Childhood Education: What We Know vs. What We Do by Michael Gramling

I'm OK! Building Resilience through Physical Play by Jarrod Green

Including One, Including All: A Guide to Relationship-Based Early Childhood Inclusion by Leslie Roffman and Todd Wanerman

Making It Better: Activities for Children Living in a Stressful World, Second Edition, by Barbara Oehlberg

So This Is Normal Too? Second Edition, by Deborah Hewitt

References

References with an asterisk indicate recommended readings.

Ainsworth, Mary, Mary C. Blehar, Everett Waters, and Sally N. Wall. 1978. *Patterns of Attachment: A Psychological Study of the Strange Situation.* Hillsdale, NJ: Erlbaum.

*American Council on the Teaching of Foreign Languages. 2011. *Benefits of Being Bilingual.* file:///Users/user/Desktop/Benefits%20of%20Language%20Learning%20-%20 American%20Council%20on%20the%20Teaching%20of%20Foreign%20Languages. webarchive.

Bowlby, John 1982. *Attachment and Loss, Vol. 1: Attachment.* New York: Basic Books.

*Buhs, Eric S., Gary W. Ladd, and Sarah L. Herald-Brown. 2010. "Victimization and Exclusion: Links to Peer Rejection, Classroom Engagement, and Achievement." In *Handbook of Bullying in Schools: An International Perspective,* edited by Shane R. Jimerson, Susan M. Swearer, and Dorothy L. Espelage. New York: Routledge.

*Cairone, Karen. 2016. "Helping Teachers Take the Challenge Out of Behavior." *Exchange Magazine.* May/June: 32–37.

*Cairone, Karen B., and Mary Mackrain. 2012. *Promoting Resilience in Preschoolers: A Strategy Guide for Early Childhood Professionals*, 2nd ed. Lewisville, NC: Kaplan.

*Carlson, Frances M. 2011. *Big Body Play: Why Boisterous, Vigorous, and Very Physical Play Is Essential to Children's Development and Learning.* Washington, DC: National Association for the Education of Young Children.

Carlsson-Paige, Nancy, and Diane E. Levin. 1992. "Making Peace in Violent Times: A Constructivist Approach to Conflict Resolution." *Young Children* 48 (1): 4–13.

*CDF (Children's Defense Fund). 2015. *The State of America's Children: 2015.* Washington, DC: Children's Defense Fund.

Cole, Layna, and Dan Gartrell. 2014. "Guidance Matters: Guidance with Girls." *Young Children* 69 (5): 94–95. www.naeyc.org/yc/columns/guidance.

*Copple, Carol, and Sue Bredekamp. 2009. *Developmentally Appropriate Practice in Early Childhood Programs Serving Children from Birth through Age 8*, 3rd ed. Washington, DC: National Association for the Education of Young Children.

Cozolino, Louis. 2006. *The Neuroscience of Human Relationships: Attachment and the Developing Social Brain.* New York: W. W. Norton.

CPI (Crisis Prevention Institute). 2012. "Managing the Crisis Moment." Brookfield, WI: National Crisis Prevention Institute.

Crawford, Patricia A., and Vicky Zygouris-Coe. 2006. "All in the Family: Connecting Home and School with Family Literacy." *Early Childhood Education Journal* 33 (4): 261–67.

*Derman-Sparks, Louise, and Julie Olsen Edwards. 2010. *Anti-Bias Education for Young Children and Ourselves.* Washington, DC: National Association for the Education of Young Children.

DeVries, Rheta, and Betty Zan. 2003. "When Children Make Rules." *Educational Leadership* 61 (1): 22–29.

Dewey, John. 1966. *Democracy and Education*. New York: Free Press.

———. 1997. *Experience and Education*. New York: Touchstone.

Dinwiddie, Sue A. 1994. "The Saga of Sally, Sammy, and the Red Pen: Facilitating Children's Social Problem Solving." *Young Children* 49 (5): 13–19.

Elliott, Rebecca. 2003. "Executive Functions and Their Disorders: Imaging in Clinical Neuroscience." *British Medical Bulletin* 65 (1): 49–59. http://bmb.oxfordjournals.org /content/65/1/49.full.pdf+html.

Epstein, Joyce L. 2001. *School, Family, and Community Partnerships: Preparing Educators and Improving Schools*. Boulder, CO: Westview.

Erikson, Erik H. 1963. *Childhood and Society*. New York: W. W. Norton.

Ettekal, Idean, and Gary W. Ladd. 2009. "The Stability of Aggressive Behavior toward Peers as a Predictor of Externalizing Problems from Childhood through Adolescence." In *Handbook of Aggressive Behavior Research*, edited by Caitriona Quinn and Scott Tawse. Hauppauge, NY: Nova Science Publishers.

*———. 2015. "Developmental Pathways from Childhood Aggression-Disruptiveness, Chronic Peer Rejection, and Deviant Friendships to Early Adolescent Rule Breaking." *Child Development* 86 (2): 614–31. doi:10.1111/cdev.12321.

Gartrell, Dan. 2000. *What the Kids Said Today: Using Classroom Conversations to Become a Better Teacher*. St. Paul, MN: Redleaf Press.

———. 2006. "Guidance Matters: The Beauty of Class Meetings." *Young Children* 61 (5): 54–55. www.naeyc.org/yc/columns/guidance.

———. 2006b. "Guidance Matters: The Beauty of Class Meetings." *Young Children* 61 (6): 54–55. www.naeyc.org/files/yc/ file/200611/BTJGuidance.pdf.

———. 2007. "Guidance Matters: 'You Really Worked Hard on Your Picture!' Guiding with Encouragement." *Young Children* 62 (3): 50–52. www.naeyc.org/yc/columns/guidance.

———. 2008. "Guidance Matters: Comprehensive Guidance." *Young Children* 63 (1): 44–45. www.naeyc.org/files/yc/file/200801/BTJGuidanceGartrell.pdf.

———. 2011a. "Guidance Matters: Reactive Aggression." *Young Children* 66 (1): 58–60. www.naeyc.org/yc/columns/guidance.

———. 2011b. "Guidance Matters: Children Who Have Serious Conflicts—Part 2: Instrumental Aggression." *Young Children* 66 (4): 60–62. www.naeyc.org/yc/columns /guidance.

———. 2011c. "Aggression, the Prequel: Preventing the Need." *Young Children* 66 (5): 62–64. www.naeyc.org/yc/columns/guidance.

———. 2012a. "From Rules to Guidelines: Moving to the Positive." *Young Children*. 67 (1): 56–58. www.naeyc.org/yc/columns/guidance.

———. 2012b. *Education for a Civil Society: How Guidance with Young Children Teaches Democratic Life Skills*. Washington, DC: NAEYC.

———. 2014. *A Guidance Approach for the Encouraging Classroom*, 4th ed. Belmont, CA: Cengage/Wadsworth.

Gartrell, Dan, and Kathleen Sonsteng. 2008. "Guidance Matters: Promote Physical Activity: It's Proactive Guidance." *Young Children*. 63 (2): 51–53. www.naeyc.org/yc/columns/guidance.

Genishi, Celia. and Anne Haas Dyson. 2009. *Children, Language, and Literacy: Diverse Learners in Diverse Times*. New York: Teachers College Press.

*Gestwicki, Carol. 2015. *Home, School, and Community Relations*, 9th ed. Belmont, CA: Wadsworth/Cengage Learning.

Gilliam, Walter S. 2005. *Prekindergartners Left Behind: Expulsion Rates in State Prekindergarten Programs*. Report. New Haven, CT: Yale University Child Study Center. www.fcd-us.org/prekindergartners-left-behind-expulsion-rates-in-state-prekindergarten-programs.

Gilliam, Walter S., and Golan Shahar. 2006. "Preschool and Child Care Expulsion and Suspension: Rates and Predictors in One State." *Infants and Young Children* 19 (3): 228–45. http://ziglercenter.yale.edu/publications/Gilliam%20and%20Shahar%20-%20 2006%20Preschool%20and%20Child%20Care%20Expulsion%20and%20Suspension%20 Rates%20and%20Predictors%20in%20One%20State_251491_5379.pdf.

Ginott, Haim G. 1993. *Teacher and Child: A Book for Parents and Teachers*. New York: Scribner Paper Fiction.

Glasser, William. 1969. *Schools without Failure*. New York: Harper and Row.

Gonzalez, Norma, Luis C. Moll, and Cathy Amanti, eds. 2005. *Funds of Knowledge: Theorizing Practices in Households, Communities, and Classrooms*. Hillsdale, NJ: Erlbaum.

Gonzalez-Mena, Janet. 2006. *Diversity in Early Care and Education: Honoring Differences*. Boston: McGraw-Hill.

———. 2008. *50 Strategies for Communicating and Working with Diverse Families*. Boston: Pearson.

*Goodnough, Abby. 2010. "The Examined Life, Aged 8. Philosophical Reasoning taught in the Second Grade." *New York Times*. www.nytimes.com/2010/04/18/education/edlife/18philosophy-t.html?ref=edlifeand_r=0.

Greenberg, Polly. 1988. "Avoiding 'Me Against You' Discipline." *Young Children* 43 (1): 24–25.

The Greta Horwitz Center. 2016. "All Feelings Are Welcome: Supporting Children's Resiliency in Stressful Times." *Exchange Magazine*. May–June: 40–43.

Gunnar, Megan R., Adriana Herrera, and Camelia E. Hostinar. 2009. "Stress and Early Brain Development." In *Encyclopedia on Early Childhood Development*, eds. Richard E. Tremblay, Michael Boivin, and Ray DeV. Peters. www.child-encyclopedia. com/brain/according-experts/stress-and-early-brain-development.

*Halgunseth, Linda C., Amy Peterson, Deborah R. Stark, and Shannon Moodie. 2009. *Family Engagement, Diverse Families, and Early Childhood Education Programs: An Integrated Review of the Literature*. Washington, DC: NAEYC and the Pew Charitable Trusts.

Harlow, Steven D. 1975. *Special Education: The Meeting of Differences*. Grand Forks, ND: University of North Dakota.

Harris, Teresa T., and Diane Fuqua. 2000. "What Goes Around Comes Around: Building a Community of Learners through Circle Times." *Young Children* 55 (1): 44–47.

Hendrick, Joanne. 1992. "Where Does It All Begin? Teaching the Principles of Democracy in the Early Years." *Young Children* 47 (3): 51–53.

Hymes, James L. 1974. *Effective Home-School Relations*. Sierra Madre, CA: Southern California Association for the Education of Young Children.

*Hyson, Marilou, and Heather Biggar Tomlinson. 2014. *The Early Years Matter: Education, Care, and the Well-Being of Children, Birth to 8*. New York: Teachers College Press/ Washington DC: NAEYC.

*Kaiser, Barbara, and Judy Sklar Rasminsky. 2016. *Challenging Behavior in Young Children: Understanding, Preventing, and Responding Effectively*, 4th ed. Boston, MA: Pearson.

Kersey, Katharine C., and Marie L. Masterson. 2009. "Teachers Connecting with Families— In the Best Interest of Children." *Young Children* 64 (6): 34–38.

King, M. 2012. "Guidance with Boys in Early Childhood Education." In Dan Gartrell, *The Power of Guidance*. Washington, DC: NAEYC.

Kriete, Roxann, and Carol Davis. 2014. *The Morning Meeting Book*, 3rd ed. Turner's Falls, MA: Northeast Foundation for Children.

Ladd, Gary W. 2006. "Peer Rejection, Aggressive or Withdrawn Behavior, and Psychological Maladjustment from Ages 5 to 12: An Examination of Four Predictive Models." *Child Development* 77 (4): 822–46.

———. 2008. "Social Competence and Peer Relations: Significance for Young Children and Their Service Providers." *Early Childhood Services* 2 (3): 129–48.

Levin Diane E. 2003. "Beyond Banning War and Superhero Play: Meeting Children's Needs in Violent Times." *Young Children* 58 (3): 60–63.

Locke, B. 1919. "Manufacturers Indorse [*sic*] the Kindergarten." *Kindergarten Circular No. 4* (July). Washington, DC: Department of the Interior, Bureau of Education.

*Lubit, Roy H. 2010. "Post-Traumatic Stress Disorder in Children." Updated June 5, 2010. Medscape. www.emedicine.medscape.com/article/918844-treatment.

Manger, T. F. 1980. "The Melting Pot and Language Maintenance in South Slavic Immigrant Groups. In *Perspectives on American English*, ed. J. L. Dillard. The Hague, The Netherlands: Mouton.

*Martin, Gerin, and Sandy Slack. 2015. *Make Room for Boys! Helping Boys Thrive in Preschool*. Ypsilanti, MI: HighScope Press.

Maslow, Abraham H. 1962. *Toward a Psychology of Being*. Princeton, NJ: Van Nostrand.

McClurg, Lois G. 1998. "Building an Ethical Community in the Classroom: Community Meeting. *Young Children* 53 (2): 30–35.

*NAEYC (National Association for the Education of Young Children). 2009. "Developmentally Appropriate Practice in Early Childhood Programs Serving Children from Birth through Age 8." Position statement. www.naeyc.org/positionstatments/dap.

*Nemeth, Karen. 2012. "Enhancing Practice with Infants and Toddlers from Diverse Language and Cultural Backgrounds." *Young Children* 67 (4): 49–57.

Pappano, Laura. 2007. "Meeting of the Minds." *Harvard Education Letter* 23 (4): 1–3.

PBIS (Positive Behavioral Interventions and Supports). 2016. "PBIS Home Page" Accessed 2017. www.pbis.org.

Pollack, William. 2001. *Real Boys Workbook: The Definitive Guide to Understanding and Interacting with Boys of All Ages*. New York: Villard Books.

President's Council on Physical Fitness and Sports, National Association for Sport and Physical Education, and Kellogg Company. 2003. *Kids in Action: Fitness for Children Birth to Age Five*. Booklet. www.fitness.gov/funfit/kidsinaction.htm.

Preuesse, Kathy. 2002. "Guidance and Discipline Strategies for Young Children: Time Out Is Out." *Early Childhood News*, March/April 12–16.

Quiocho, Alice, and Annette M. Daoud. 2006. "Dispelling Myths about Latino Parent Participation in Schools." *The Educational Forum* 70: 255–67.

Readdick, Christine A., and Paula L. Chapman. 2000. "Young Children's Perceptions of Time Out." *Journal of Research in Childhood Education* 15 (1): 81–87.

Reineke, Jane, Kathleen Sonsteng, and Dan Gartrell. 2008. "Viewpoint. Nurturing Mastery Motivation: No Need for Rewards." *Young Children* 63 (6): 89, 93–77.

Rogers, Carl R. 1961. *On Becoming a Person*. Boston: Houghton Mifflin.

Sanders, Stephen W. 2002. *Active for Life: Developmentally Appropriate Movement Programs for Young Children*. Washington DC: Human Kinetics Publishers.

Schott Foundation for Public Education. 2015. "Black Lives Matter: The Schott 50 State Report on Public Education and Black Males" in Education Week's Blogs, February 11. http://blogs.edweek.org/edweek/District_Dossier/2015/02/as_nation_graduation_rate _grew.html.

Schreiber, Mary. E. 1999. "Timeouts for Toddlers: Is Our Goal Punishment or Education?" *Young Children* 54 (4): 22–25.

*Schwartz, Casey. 2011. "Why It's Smart to Be Bilingual." *Newsweek*. August 7. www .thedailybeast.com/newsweek/2011/08/07/why-it-s-smart-to-be-bilingual.html.

Shin, Hyon B. and Robert A. Kominksi. 2010. *Language Use in the United States: 2007*. American Community Survey Reports, United States Census Bureau.

Shonkoff, Jack P. and Andrew S. Garner. 2011. "The Lifelong Effects of Early Childhood Adversity and Toxic Stress." *Pediatrics* 129 (1). http://pediatrics.aappublications.org /content/early/2011/12/21/peds.2011-2663.full.pdf.

Snyder, Thomas D. 1993. *120 Years of American Education: A Statistical Portrait*. National Center for Education Statistics.

Souto-Manning, Mariana, and Kevin J. Swick. 2006. "Teachers' Beliefs about Parent and Family Involvement: Rethinking Our Family Involvement Paradigm." *Early Childhood Education Journal* 34 (2): 187–93.

Sperry, Rachel. 2011. *FLIP IT*®*: Transforming Challenging Behavior*. Lewisville, NC: Kaplan Early Learning.

Teaching for Change. 2016. "Anti-Bias Education." www.teachingforchange.org /teacher-resources/anti-bias-education.

US Department of Education. 2015. "US High School Graduation Rate Hits New Record High." February 12.

*Vance, Emily. 2015. *Class Meetings: Young Children Solving Problems Together*. rev. ed. Washington, DC: NAEYC.

Vance, Emily, and Patricia J. Weaver. 2002. *Class Meetings: Young Children Solving Problems Together.* Washington, DC: NAEYC.

Wartenberg, Thomas. 2009. *Big Ideas for Little Kids: Teaching Philosophy through Children's Literature.* Washington DC: Rowman and Littlefield.

*Watson, Marilyn. 2003. "Attachment Theory and Challenging Behaviors: Reconstructing the Nature of Relationships." *Young Children* 58 (4): 12–20.

Weber S, U. Habel, K. Amunts, and F. Schneider. 2008. "Structural Brain Abnormalities in Psychopaths—A Review." *Behavioral Sciences and the Law* 26 (1): 7–28.

Weber-Schwartz, Nancy. 1987. "Patience or Understanding." *Young Children* 42 (3): 52–54.

Westbrook, Robert B. 1995. *John Dewey and American Education.* Ithaca, NY: Cornell University Press.

Wien, Carol Anne. 2004. "From Policing to Participation: Overturning the Rules and Creating Amiable Classrooms." *Young Children* 59 (1): 34–40.

Williford, Anne, and Kathryn J. Depaolis. 2012. "Identifying Predictors of Instrumental and Reactive Aggression among Low-Income Minority Adolescent Girls." *Journal of the Society for Social Work and Research* 3 (3): 145–61.

*York, Stacey. 2016. *Roots and Wings: Affirming Culture and Preventing Bias in Early Childhood.* 3rd ed. St. Paul, MN: Redleaf Press.

Index

CPSIA information can be obtained
at www.ICGtesting.com
Printed in the USA
JSHW022053150320
4698JS00002BA/6

9 781605 545370